"WHAT'S THE DIFFERENCE BETWEEN 'SOUND' ADVICE AND 'SOUNDS GOOD' ADVICE? HOW **DO YOU DISCERN THE DIFFERENCE**?"

—PHIL BODINE

What Financial Gear Are You In?

PHIL BODINE

Copyedited & Produced by:
Jennifer Edwards | jedwardsediting.net

Cover Design, Interior Book Design & Typography by:
Linné Garrett | 829 DESIGN | 829Design.com

401(k) illustration by Shaelin Sullivan | 829 DESIGN

"Lucky The Mouse" photo by Craig Orsini. Used with permission.

Scripture verse marked TLB comes from The Living Bible, copyright © 1971 by Tyndale House Foundation. Used by permission of Tyndale House Publishers Inc., Carol Stream, Illinois 60188.

Library of Congress Control Number: 2024915952

PRINTED IN THE UNITED STATES OF AMERICA

Endorsements

Phil's book obviously has a lifetime of learning in it. I know many advisors who work in this space, and he stands out as one of the most humble and growth-oriented advisors I know. I was so honored to get to read an advance copy of *Wealth in Overdrive*® and thrilled to see how helpful it will be for those who want the full story in today's world of three-second sound bites.

—**Kim Butler, prosperityeconomics.org**
Author of *Busting the Financial Planning Lies* and *Perpetual Wealth*;
Kim's work has been recommended by financial thought leaders and
authors such as Robert Kiyosaki *(Rich Dad Poor Dad)*, Tom Wheelwright
(Tax-Free Wealth), and Garrett Gunderson *(Killing Sacred Cows)*

Opportunity comes at the intersection of people and places. As long as you are always putting yourself in the right places and in front of the right people, opportunity knocks. Phil is one of those right people, and if you are holding this book, you are in the right place. Now it is up to you to execute what this book says, the way Phil says to do it.

—**Bryan S. Bloom, CPA**
Author of *Confessions of a CPA*

Phil does an outstanding job laying out wise decisions around your financial future. I really appreciate that this book focuses on good, sound financial decisions to help build efficient and optimal wealth and legacy over time. Thank you for focusing on teaching financial wisdom vs. allowing other external sources to make those decisions for me.

—**Dan Fachner**
CEO/Chairman of the Board for J&J Snack Foods Corp,
ICEE® and Dippin' Dots®

This book may rock your financial, family, and future vision. Plus, you may be shocked about what you learn about forgiveness. I could not stop reading this book, and I suspect you'll do the same. Buckle up and get ready for Overdrive!

—**Dr. John Jackson**
Author of *Grace Ambassador,* William Jessup University President,
Writer/Speaker on Leadership and Transformation

This book is not your typical financial book in any way. It is filled with experienced wisdom and vital strategies to enhance and enrich your life. Intelligent, inciteful, and relevant. Be prepared to be educated and inspired, but most importantly … to take action!

—**Dave Dias**
Chairman of the Board, FoundationsOfFreedom.com

If you are looking for a comprehensive guide that will help you make informed decisions about your financial future, then look no further than *Wealth in Overdrive®*. This remarkable book is a game changer for anyone seeking to protect their loved ones, grow their knowledge of rarely explained planning strategies, and create long-term generational wealth for their family. Whether you're a beginner or a seasoned investor, this book will revolutionize the way you think about Money. I know from personal experience. I hope that everyone will buy this book, learn from Phil's expert insights, and leverage this knowledge to make well-informed financial decisions.

—**Scott McGuckin**
Human Resources Manager for a Fortune 100 Company

NAVIGATING ONE'S FINANCIAL FUTURE REQUIRES REFERENCE OF INFORMATION TO ENABLE ONE'S CHOICES TO BEAR FRUIT. SUCH A REFERENCE IS THIS TIMELY BOOK BY PHIL—SHARING CHOICES TO RECEIVE FINANCIAL RESULTS DESIRED.

—**Richard King Brown**
Life Insurance Professional

In a world of financial scammers and buffoons, Phil Bodine stands out as a skilled man of integrity with an earnest passion for helping others. I know from firsthand experience. The financial, spiritual, and relational wisdom he disperses throughout *Wealth in Overdrive*® can change the trajectory of your life. He takes what is often complicated and makes it easy to understand, and therein lies the man's genius.

Phil has a proven track record of success for his clients, stemming from a life of dedication to his craft. What you will learn in this invaluable book will change how you think about money forever and help you attain the financial freedom to do what you were born to do.

—**Zoro**
World-renowned drummer for Lenny Kravitz, Bobby Brown,
Frankie Valli, New Edition, author of *Maria's Scarf: A Memoir of a
Mother's Love, a Son's Perseverance & Dreaming Big*

Wealth in Overdrive® changed my perspective on managing the money I've worked so hard to attain. This book is easy to understand and applies to everyone. I've recommended *Wealth in Overdrive*® strategies to teenagers just starting their careers, people closing in on retirement, business owners, and everyone in between.

I wish every industry had a Phil Bodine—someone committed to exposing the fallacies within their industry while at the same time providing sensible advice that everyone benefits from.

—**Jud Boies**
Executive Director/Founder of Business Goals, author of *Goals*
and *The Church Quiz*. Business Goals has reached over a million people
around the world over the past 25 years

Dedication

I dedicate this book to my wife, Carin,
our children, grandchildren,
and future great-grandchildren.
Thank you for allowing me to
live out the legacy of my father,
William C. Bodine.

At Wealth in Overdrive®, We Believe:

THAT EVERYONE we encounter has a greater wealth potential than the current track they are on to achieve.

WE ALSO BELIEVE Wall Street and financial institutions have fed people false information and flawed formulas, which, along with eroding threats in the economy, have actually prevented them from achieving their optimum potential.

WE EXIST TO HELP our clients overcome those obstacles and make progress toward their full wealth-building and retirement income potential, while preserving the financial integrity of their family.

CONTENTS

WARNING!

Do not be misled by the title of this book ...

Wealth in Overdrive® is not a matter of what gear YOU are in.

Rather, it's a matter of what financial gear your MONEY is in.

Everyone makes money. The BIGGER question is, how many people keep the money that they earn?

The answer is very few. That's why you need a financial advisor who understands how to protect and preserve the money you earn.

THAT WOULD BE PHIL BODINE.

Who do you turn to for financial advice? The important question is how accurate is their advice? But the critical question is, how does their advice impact your wealth?

Phil studies and understands money. He knows how to save it, he knows how to invest it, and he knows the most important part ... how to keep it.

Think about your money for a moment ...

Do you have enough? Probably not.

Are you paying the least amount of taxes (legally)? Probably not.

Are you squeezing every last drop out of every dollar you earn? Probably not.

Is your money secure? Probably not.

Is your retirement income enough? Probably not.

Is your plan in place to end your work career and enjoy the next phase? Probably not.

Have you taken advantage of every legal tax benefit? Probably not.

IN THIS BOOK, PHIL PROVIDES MONEY AND WEALTH INSIGHT ... But he also shows his human and ethical side—Midwestern values. That's the **Bodine Difference**. Phil cares about the person and their desired outcomes FIRST ... then creates an exclusive tailored plan to make it happen.

When you read the core principles that overflow into Phil's life and his business, you will fully understand the depth of his financial genius. AND, after you read and comprehend these nine core principles of financial success, he immediately challenges you to compare his to yours.

Phil's words are not just thought-provoking, he challenges you to think deeper and take action. In his first tip, he doesn't just ask you what you're wanting—he challenges you to think WHY you want it. Brilliant!

Phil's insight is frighteningly accurate.

Take a look at "the 8 most common unintended financial mistakes." Here, Phil lets you take a look at yourself to identify where you may be taking the wrong steps. Powerful information and a mega-dose of reality. But there is more ...

When you understand the difference between a scarcity mindset and abundance, you at once understand how Phil will help you acquire and keep your wealth. This is genuine gold!

And you will be challenged to understand and implement the difference between knowing and DOING ... Phil knows you may know it but asks, "Are you doing it?" and "At what level?"

This book is not optional—it's mandatory. It's imperative that you understand your money so that you can keep it in a way that fortifies you and your family for generations to come.

Wealth in Overdrive® examines every element of money, including earning, risking, acquiring, and keeping your wealth.

This book is **bold**, this book is **brilliant**, this book is **bankable**, and this book is based on facts, not theory. In short, this book is **Badass Wealth!**

I feel blessed to be able to write this foreword because this book contains the answers that you're looking for. And it's my goal to provide both understanding and challenge to Phil's wisdom.

This book must be read more than once, underlined, and studied. Especially those elements that relate to you and your personal philosophy about the practical use of money. Your money.

Please take advantage of Phil's life journey to acquire the wealth you desire and keep the wealth you've worked so hard for.

Wealth in Overdrive® will give you the action steps you need to take, PLUS the peace of mind you need to continue to work at your peak performance—the financial peace of mind that you have earned and deserve.

—Jeffrey Gitomer,
Author of New York Times Best-Selling
Little Red Book of Selling and *The Little Gold Book of YES! Attitude*

Acknowledgments

I heard a story once about a man who entered his donkey in the Kentucky Derby. When questioned about this, the man replied, "Oh, I don't expect him to win, but I thought the association would do him good."

I have relied heavily on others during the creation of this book. I have enjoyed the association with some world-class people, and I would like to express my appreciation to many of them.

Before anyone else, I want to thank my wife, Carin, who has been indispensable throughout this long and lengthy process. She has played every role a person can play in the writing of this book: spouse, friend, babysitter, cheerleader, critic, and probably most importantly, therapist. It is no exaggeration to say this book would not be the same without her, and it might not even exist at all.

...

Secondly, Robbie Sondag, for sensing my frustration when asking, "How is the book project going?" Then, taking on the daunting task of completely transforming and rewriting the entire book to flow and capture each page to sound more like me all while still retaining my original message! Forever grateful!!!

...

Nigel Templeman, my sounding board, gave me the affirmation I needed when I needed it, without either one of us fully appreciating or knowing how much I needed it. Your notes of criticism, praise, analysis, feedback, patience, and countless hours of dedication meant everything to the completion of this project.

...

Vanessa Mohammed, it is wonderful for Carin and me to have a person in our lives who not only can run our "professional universe" but does it with a positive attitude, a servant mindset, grace, and an "over-pleasing personality" to the clients we serve. You are truly remarkable!

...

Thank you to the many people who read early versions of the manuscript: Jud Boies, Kim Butler, Larry and Lori Hill, RKB, Zoro, Vicki Newman, Marissa Cardozo, Abigail Neeley, and Jason Fagan. The book has benefited greatly from your feedback.

To my mentors: college volleyball coach Arnie Ball, thank you for giving me a chance and believing in my talents and abilities. I not only stumbled on to a college degree, but it changed the trajectory of my life. Robert Castiglione, you expanded my mind, gave me insight, and helped me better understand the principles of Macroeconomics to personal finance through the Lifetime Economic Acceleration Process. Richard King Brown, you have been a source of Inspiration, Truth, and Wisdom.

•••

Instructors: Robert Castiglione, Art and Jason Sanger, Kim Butler, Todd Langford, Al Dickens, Vincent D'Addona, MSFS, CLU®, ChFC®, CEXP®, RICP®, AEP®, Lucian Ioja, Ande Frazier, CFP®, CLU®, ChFC®, RICP®, Mike Steranka, Keith Chapman, Don Blanton, and Jeffrey Gitomer.

•••

Randomly, in no order, thanks to the many advisors and colleagues that I've known and become close friends with who have challenged me to be the best advisor I can be: Jamie Chesser, Ian Meierdiercks, Brucie Weinstein, Scott Lauer, Caleb Guilliams, Chris Mann, CPA, CFP®, Steve McCormick, CPA, John L. Smallwood, CFP®, CLU®, ChFC®, Mike Romanello, Dave Dias, Wayne Allen, Esq., Brian LaRoche, Vlad Donets, Steven Wright AIF®, Edward Cotney, Michael Sollazzo, Esq., Bryan Bloom, CPA, Paul Robb, CFP®, CLU®, ChFC®, Nick Robb, Trent Fortner, Jim Lilley, Brian Bole, and Elizabeth Dawson.

•••

To all my clients we serve and friends who persistently stayed on me to not only start this book project but cheered me on till the end!

•••

To my editor, Jennifer Edwards, through ten edits and drafts, giving careful attention to detail and the ability to diplomatically rein in excerpts burst of passion (and sometimes irritation) in many drafts made for a much more measured and balanced book. Your endless patience gave me the space I needed to create a book I was proud of and championed my ideas at every step.

•••

Linné Garrett of 829 DESIGN, I appreciate your professionalism and your eye for artistry and detail. I couldn't be happier with the way this book turned out.

•••

To my Dad, I MISS YOU! If only I could fill one of your shoes, I would be a true success in life!

•••

The Man on the Middle Cross who sacrificed his life for me so that I might live.

WHAT FINANCIAL GEAR ARE YOU IN?
(DON'T SKIP THIS PART!)

When I was growing up, I always wondered, *What do rich people know that I don't?* I knew they dressed differently, owned better cars, and lived in nicer homes than I did. But I was curious about the knowledge aspect, which made me continually ponder not only that question but also how money really works.

Over time, I discovered there is no clear-cut road map to wealth being taught in our schools and universities. Nor do parents typically engage in open discussions about money. Even more regrettably, the minority who do talk about it with their kids typically don't have the correct answers or the right education themselves.

I would guess that most people tend to manage money based on what they observed with their own families as they grew up during their formative years. While IRA plans and early home payoff approaches are standard practices used by many these days, these options aren't really designed to build true wealth.

In fact, the most common methods tend to revolve around purchasing financial products instead of thinking through sound financial strategies.

I've spent the majority of my adult life pursuing the reasons behind most of the commonly used formulas of our culture. And it's amazing what you discover when you dig past the status quo.

If you're looking for a book that will help you learn how to get rich quick, play the stock market, or pursue financial shortcuts, then congratulations! This book is *not* for you! There are already plenty of books like that on the market. Take your pick!

Honestly, I'm not sure the world really needs yet another book about finances, but it has become painfully obvious that our country has a real problem with money. And it's not just the national debt (though that is one result). *The actual dilemma is that so many people don't have a clue about how money really works, nor do they have a structured road map to get them to their desired destination.*

If you really want to understand money, you need to begin by grasping the difference between getting rich versus gaining and preserving wealth. Getting rich includes things like securing a high-paying job, winning the lottery, or inheriting a lump sum. Creating and preserving wealth, however, is different.

Wealth is about setting up a system or strategies and adopting a mindset that allows your money to live and breathe. We want to create ongoing streams of passive income. We want to truly understand how to convert each dollar into an employee who will work for you on several levels, not just one.

In our entertainment-driven, sound-bite, fast-cash society, most people aren't pursuing wealth. They're chasing riches. And there are many financial entertainers who will gladly assist you in that endeavor. But they're not teaching methods for obtaining or preserving true wealth. The truth is, most aren't even instructing you on how to get rich! They're simply selling a book, a product, or a system designed to help themselves get rich. Very rarely are principles or methods of wealth accumulation clearly and accurately explained on a more comprehensive or holistic level. Few financial books ever even delve into the heart and practicalities of money. *The good news is, this book does.*

There's an old saying that goes something like this:

"If you keep doing what you've always done, you'll keep getting what you've always gotten."

By reading this book, you will learn things about wealth and money you've never likely heard from the general public or a typical financial advisor. I'm one who challenges conventional wisdom, and you need to know upfront what you're getting into. Our culture is overflowing with systems designed to not only keep you from gaining true wealth but to hypnotically prevent you from understanding how wealth even works in the first place.

Over the past thirty years, many people have encouraged me to write this book. Yet, I've held off until now.

The reason is, I didn't know if it was really worth the time and effort. In other words, I didn't understand my WHY. What could possibly compel me to jump into such an all-encompassing endeavor?

However, when I finally sat down and listed my reasons, the floodgates began to open for me. I want to be known for serving my clients with humility and advising them to be the best possible stewards of their God-given resources while maintaining the financial integrity of their families. I became reinvigorated by my commitment to serving others in ways that can drastically change their lives, and I was so energized by what I had written that I thought it might be inspiring for you, as well. I wrote this book to:

* challenge the skeptic;

* save or impact a marriage;

* avert a financial mistake;

* demand a decision;

* conceive a dream;

* solve a problem;

* create security, confidence, and peace of mind where there is fear, tension, and insecurity;

* change the course of someone's financial future for the better;

* create and solidify a better financial game plan;

* make a financial impact;

* and create clarity for the betterment of other people's quality of life!

You can't predict what your financial plan will be years from now, but you can create a strategy to accommodate the unknown. The financial planning world is filled with all kinds of confusing and conflicting information that can leave people both wandering and wondering.

**And when people don't know what to do,
they typically don't do anything and their engine stalls.
Or they fall prey to the misleading information spewed
from financial institutions, entertainers,
and so-called advisors who "support" them.**

—Phil Bodine

Think about it! Financial institutions and advisors are in business to make a profit. If the majority of the population blindly goes along with culturally accepted plans, why should we expect "money experts" to kill the goose that lays the golden egg? That's not to say that good banks or financial advisors don't exist. But the bottom line is they are in business to make money.

Now, you might be thinking, "But Phil, my financial advisor is a good friend, and he really knows his stuff. He certainly wouldn't steer me wrong." I'm sure he is a good guy. And he probably knows his products well. But is he actually teaching you wealth strategies and aligning your values, or simply adding to his own portfolio?

Has financial advice ever made you feel like you're walking through life with a cardboard box over your head?

"IF YOU SEEK THE COUNSEL OF **100 DIFFERENT** FINANCIAL **ADVISORS**, YOU'LL LIKELY WALK AWAY WITH **100** COMPLETELY **DIFFERENT PLANS**. AND THE FUNNY THING IS, EACH ONE OF THESE PROFESSIONALS WOULD BE **COMPLETELY CONVINCED THEIR PLAN IS** THE BEST."

—PHIL BODINE

Let's be honest. There is a plethora of misleading information, paralysis of choices, and conflicting viewpoints coming from so many different places that it's hard to know what to believe. Accountants say one thing, attorneys say another, not to mention the things your investment advisor, banker, and insurance broker say—then there's your family and friends, the guy at the coffee shop, and your golf partner! **NOISE CREATES CONFUSION**. Everyone has a personal opinion. Magazines and newspaper articles, media and news reports, white papers, *The Wall Street Journal*, and financial entertainers are chock-full of conflicting "words of wisdom." How is the average person supposed to make sense of it all? How do you discern the difference between "sound" advice vs. "sounds good" advice?

If you seek the counsel of one hundred different financial advisors, you'll likely walk away with one hundred completely different plans. And the funny thing is, each one of these financial professionals would be completely convinced their plan is the best.

Unfortunately, most people are so confused or overwhelmed by the sheer amount of information available that they'll settle for anything that remotely makes sense. They simply want to be able to say, "I'm good. I've got a financial planner. I've got my guy. He takes care of me. He knows what's going on."

But what I want to know is, "Do YOU know what's going on with YOUR money?" No one should care more about your money than YOU! That's why it baffles me that so many people want to take the easy way out. It's almost like they don't really want to know what's going on. They say, "Just tell me what I need." "How much is it?" "Just manage it for me." "I trust you. After all, you're the expert. You work at a bank. You have to know what you're doing, right?"

Oh, I guarantee you they know what they're doing! But wouldn't it be better to have your own basic grasp on financial scenarios so you can begin to make educated decisions based on your values and what's most important to you and your family? Having a product isn't enough, and just having information isn't enough. It's having the wisdom, understanding, strategies, and a game plan to know what to do with that information that matters.

My ultimate goal in writing this book is to heighten your financial awareness and give you a vantage point that most people rarely see.

I want to help you defeat yesterday's understanding of how wealth works and move you forward toward your own success story.

You'll see that Chapters 1–12 break down some of the most common financial problems and misconceptions simply by looking at them from a new vantage point. Then, in Chapter 13, I will reveal a pathway I call "The Solution" that I'm certain you'll never hear from 99% of the other financial advisors in the industry. I think it will rock your world.

By reading this book, I will give you the keys and a road map to true wealth that works *for* you and helps you accomplish your goals and dreams. However, you're the one who has to start the car and stay the course. **You can plan for then, NOW!** Once you do that, you'll be well on your way to shifting your *Wealth into Overdrive*®.

The only thing worse than being blind is having sight but no vision.

—Helen Keller

"AT WEALTH IN OVERDRIVE®, WE HELP BRING **THE** *FUTURE* TO THE **PRESENT**, SO YOU CAN FIX IT NOW."

—NIGEL TEMPLEMAN

THE QUIZ

WHAT FINANCIAL GEAR ARE YOU IN?

TAKE THIS QUIZ TO FIND OUT

Like with any new endeavor, it's important to understand what you know and what you don't know to create a baseline of knowledge. I'm going to ask you to take a quick quiz designed to assess your current financial mental capacity (i.e., the "financial gear" you are in). I've asked many people to take it over the years, and they are always surprised at what they thought they knew but didn't. Don't worry; this is not meant to embarrass you—no one but you will see your answers. It's simply meant to gauge where you are regarding the basics of money and wealth.

Look at the ten questions below and try to answer them to the best of your knowledge. Don't overthink them. They are not trick questions. And don't fret if you honestly don't know an answer. Just give it a shot. I'd like you to use a pen or pencil and mark "True" or "False" for each question—don't just answer them in your head.

FINANCIAL GEAR **QUIZ**

This quiz is a crucial starting point for developing a more intentional financial game plan. Good luck!

TRUE   FALSE

○   ○   **1.** Insurance companies want you to have the lowest deductible possible on your auto and homeowners insurance.

○   ○   **2.** A 15-year mortgage will save you more money over time than a 30-year mortgage.

○   ○   **3.** Term life insurance has the highest overall cost to you, the insured, over your life expectancy.

○   ○   **4.** You will be in a lower tax bracket at retirement.

○   ○   **5.** Tax deferrals, like IRAs and 401(k)s, are the most efficient way to accumulate wealth.

TRUE	FALSE		
○	○	**6.**	Life insurance is a good investment.
○	○	**7.**	The rate of return on home equity depends on the location of the home.
○	○	**8.**	A life insurance company allows you to borrow from your life insurance contract.
○	○	**9.**	Given the insured's age and the size of the desired death benefit, the life insurance company determines the maximum amount of premium to be paid.
○	○	**10.**	A life insurance company is buying your risk when you purchase a life insurance contract.

So, what financial gear do you think you are in? First gear, you haven't left the driveway yet. You want a financial plan, but you don't know where to start. Second gear: you're going down a back-street or an alley. You are practicing some financial saving principles, but you're just getting started. Third gear: you're committed to a plan. You've got a mortgage and a retirement plan, and you are contributing to an investment portfolio, but you don't know where you are headed. You're driving around in circles. And then there is overdrive, where you are now on the autobahn, and your financial engine is running on all cylinders.

Believe it or not, many financial professionals don't get these answers all right. They think they are in overdrive, but they're using practices that are keeping them stuck in second or third gear. I think you'll find as you read this book there are ideas you've never thought of or have misunderstood that can help you get your financial engine working more efficiently for you.

I know that most of the time, whenever you take a quiz, the answer key is close by and the idea is to get a rating on how well you did. But rather than just give you the answers now, I want this book to teach you the reasons for the answers. I want to explain the specific strategies, principles, and concepts that will make each answer obvious by the time you're done with the book. And when you retake the quiz in Chapter 18, I'm confident you'll get a perfect score. More importantly, you'll understand the WHY behind the answers and be able to finetune and calibrate your financial engine to achieve its highest performance.

WHO IS THIS GUY?

You may be thinking . . .

Who in the world is Phil Bodine, and why should I trust him? He just called into question the methods and motives of our most typical and widely accepted financial beliefs. What makes him different than other financial advisors and professionals? How did he end up with this "super knowledge" he claims is so rare to the general public? And why would he even share these wealth secrets in the first place?

That's what I'd be wondering, too, if I were you. And those are great questions! Let me start by sharing a little about my background—not just my credentials; I'm talking about my life from the beginning—how I got to where I am with the view of money I have.

I grew up in a blue-collar family in Fort Wayne, Indiana, in the 1960s. My dad was a second-shift factory worker at General Motors, and he also owned a painting business on the side. He and my mother didn't teach me how to make money; they taught me and my four brothers how to work hard, live with integrity, and look out for those in need.

With regard to working hard, I was taught:

* Be on time—by football coach Vince Lombardi's time rules:

  → If you're fifteen minutes early, you're "on time."

  → If you're on time, you're late.

  → If you're ten minutes late, you're rude and disrespectful of others' time.

* Finish what you started.

* Do more than what is expected of you.

* Have a good attitude.

* Put things back where you found them (especially my dad's tools).

* If you helped create the mess, you can help clean it up. Leave things better off than how you found them.

* Be grateful for everything and feel entitled to nothing.

* Get your work done first before play, not the other way around.

As far as living with integrity, I learned:

* It's important to do the right thing for the right reason.

* **NOTHING** in life is free.
* Do what you say you're going to do … your word is your bond.
* A handshake is a contract.
* Treat others better than they treat you.
* Do things right or don't do them at all.
* Never do or say anything that you'll have to go back and apologize for.
* Family is everything.

But most importantly, I was taught to look out for those in need:

* Put God first.
* Put others before yourself.
* Contribute part of your income to charity.
* Be a good steward of your God-given resources.
* Get to give versus give to get … give without expecting anything in return.
* Understand the importance of not measuring or keeping score, and give from the heart.

And I'll be honest. Many families in the Midwest lived that way during that time period. However, I believe it was my father's example that made the biggest impact on my life and how I live today. My father was a man of great faith and integrity who truly believed God would provide, especially during tough times.

I remember the first time I ever saw my dad cry. It was after he was laid off. I'm sure that was a humbling moment for him, yet as a family, we did what we needed to do to make ends meet. That meant we ate lots of garden-grown tomato-and-mayo sandwiches, and at times, we'd have cereal for dinner. But no matter how tough things got, Dad never wavered from his faith. He truly believed God would take care of us. And regardless of how tight things were, Dad never stopped giving or believing.

Regular giving was embedded in his DNA. He taught us that we couldn't out give God. We were to be good stewards of our resources and money, regardless of the size of our income. And when you develop a lifestyle of continually serving others, it takes your mind off yourself. Suddenly, your own problems don't seem quite so bad. In short, you become a life-giver instead of a life-taker.

My dad was a total life-giver. He would literally give the shirt off his back to help someone in need. I saw him do it time and time again. He'd give his coat to somebody who didn't have a coat. And trust me, northern Indiana has cold winters.

It wasn't uncommon for my dad to wake me up **very** early on a Saturday morning to help him with a paint job. Looking back on it now, it's clear to me that he knew in advance many were not paying gigs. We did them anyway. He considered those projects to be giving expeditions.

Though I didn't know it then, my dad was instilling values in me that would not only define his legacy but shape mine. When he died at just sixty-eight years of age, hundreds of people crammed into our little evangelical church. It was packed well beyond capacity. That day, I learned that my dad's backyard garden wasn't merely to feed our family; it was for helping and giving to others, too. He grew more cucumbers, tomatoes, and zucchini than we could have ever eaten as a family, simply to provide food to others in need.

Now, I certainly don't want to shortchange my mom. Both of my parents were instrumental in instilling the importance of hard work, integrity, and giving. But I don't really remember being taught how to make or manage money. In fact, when it came to money, the only thing I remember was we didn't have a lot of it. I never received an allowance. Vacations were virtually nonexistent. And if I wanted some spending money . . . if it was going to be, it was up to me to find odd jobs.

When you grow up in an environment where money is scarce, you learn to appreciate what you do have, almost to a fault. Holidays like Halloween were exhilarating because of the opportunity to acquire candy for *FREE!* So when I went trick-or-treating, I'd actually canvass the entire neighborhood with the goal of collecting as much candy as I possibly could. Then, I would hoard it under my bed like a squirrel. It would sit there for weeks on end. I was afraid to eat any of it because that would reduce my bounty. Unfortunately, I discovered that an untouched candy stash eventually turned into a stale candy stash, and I never got to actually enjoy it. I guess it's really true: to the victor go the spoils.

I learned the same lesson with the piggy bank I received as a birthday gift from my grandmother. She told me I could use it to store all the money I earned from helping her clean her house. I worked hard to fill it up, but I never got to enjoy my earnings because I was too scared to spend any of it. It was all part of a scarcity mindset I now call "the piggy bank syndrome." Like the Halloween candy, my money was essentially stored in a prison of my own making. No one ever really taught me the principles of money or how to get money into motion, much less how to invest, manage, or enjoy it. So whenever I acquired some, I clung to it. But the lesson I learned is that **MONEY HAS NO VALUE UNTIL IT IS EXCHANGED FOR SOMETHING OF VALUE.**

My work motivation increased dramatically when I reached the ninth grade. It was then that my parents informed me that they were going to stop buying anything for me that they deemed "non essential." They said, "We'll provide a roof over your head and food for your belly, but for everything else, you're on your own." And they meant it.

I remember how excited I was to make the varsity basketball team during my sophomore year in high school. But trying to convince my parents that I "needed" a new pair of a hundred and ten dollar Adidas leather high-top basketball shoes was another story. They considered them nonessential. Thankfully, they did contribute twenty dollars to my basketball career. But they left it up to me to creatively figure out how to raise the ninety-dollar balance. And guess what? I did! I mowed lawns, shoveled walks, raked leaves, and did whatever I could to get those high-tops. I'm convinced that no one on the basketball team appreciated their shoes more than I did. To this day, I still can't understand having or owning anything without having to earn it.

After high school, I spent ten months working for a utility company. I had no college aspirations. However, a coach observed me playing volleyball in an amateur club league, and he saw something he liked. So he lined up an opportunity for me to make it as a walk-on at Indiana/Purdue University, holding out the prospect that there might be a scholarship available to play Division I volleyball. His hunch was correct, and from my point of view, life-changing. I landed a full-ride scholarship, which was an absolute windfall and a tremendous blessing! It's the only way I could have afforded college (even with the savings from my job at the utility company). Of course, I was so green and unprepared for college that I didn't even know what to study. For some reason, learning about money seemed like a safe and sensible idea. So, I declared business as my major.

When I graduated from college in the spring of 1989, I joined a small boutique financial firm with an accountant, an attorney, a few stock brokers, money managers, and insurance brokers. It was there I began to notice the distinct strategies and perspectives of each of those particular specialists. I soaked it all in like a sponge. My work ethic, which I had learned at home and as a high school and college athlete, suddenly kicked into high gear. I wanted to learn as much as possible.

I was fortunate to find several wonderful mentors who encouraged me to look at money differently. They challenged me to see a broader picture of wealth accumulation and preservation and to question the conventional wisdom that promised riches but produced mediocre results.

Once I developed a more comprehensive, broader financial perspective, I was forced to re-evaluate my current position at the firm. I began to realize that I was basically doing what everyone was telling me to do. I was told what to sell and who to sell it to. And it sometimes traced back to what was best for the firm, not the client.

As I watched this play out over and over again, I rationalized this behavior. Of course, why wouldn't we do business in this manner? After all, we wanted to make a profit. The clients were just along for the ride. We weren't mean or unethical. We were just following typical bottom-line strategies adopted by many of the household advisory firms on Main Street (also known as wirehouses). We'd amass clients, sell them products, and then charge them a percentage of their assets as an ongoing fee.

But something didn't seem right about this process. The general public's lack of financial intelligence, combined with the high trust factor they placed in us as professionals, was the perfect recipe for making a profit at their expense. And even though I was young in the business, it seemed to me like there had to be a better way for both the client and the firm to win. It had to be a win-win scenario, in that order.

But what was I supposed to do? Buck the system? Rock the boat? Ultimately, I returned to a very simple principle I was raised on: **do the right thing for the right reason.** To me, that meant putting the customer first. I wanted to help each individual develop a comprehensive wealth plan that would become a solid foundation for a successful future. I wanted each plan to make sense to the client and for each client's wish list to become a reality. The client needed to understand how money worked. In short, the thing that mattered the most was **what the client wanted, not what I wanted for the client.**

I remember being in Chicago when the Trump International Hotel and Tower was under construction along the river. Standing on the Irv Kupcinet Bridge on Wabash Avenue, just a block away from the Magnificent Mile, I watched as steel girders were driven miles and miles down into the wet concrete to provide a strong foundation. It made an indelible impression on me. This amazing structure all began with that colossal foundation. Without it, it would not stand. That day, I realized that **structures don't restrict you; they strengthen you.** They allow you to build something amazing. In other words, you don't build a skyscraper on an outhouse foundation.

"STRUCTURES
DON'T
RESTRICT
YOU; THEY
STRENGTHEN
YOU."

–PHIL BODINE

The same is true when it comes to managing someone's money. Most financial advisors are great at selling products. Very few look at the big picture. It's a product-driven industry. To help a client actually lay a foundation for implementing a plan that includes all aspects of their finances (income streams, insurance, asset preservation, investments, cash flow, tax planning, debt structure, retirement, savings, and real estate purchases) is rare. Ideally, all variables should work together to achieve what the client really wants. However, just like building a custom home, it has to begin with a foundation—not a roof, not a window, and not a door.

Eventually, I decided that instead of convincing my co-workers to employ a big-picture concept, it would be better for me to branch off and lay a little foundation of my own. I wanted to build a business that provided a complete package for the client, not one that would merely sell them a product. I wanted to be an actual fiduciary, someone who prudently took care of my client's money and assets. And even more importantly, I wanted to educate my clients on how to get their money in motion.

I truly believe that people are smart enough to make their own decisions if they just understand how certain financial systems work. With all the confusing and contradictory money advice flooding the marketplace, I want to provide something different: *real answers.*

Other financial advisors may claim to make the same kind of promise, but when it comes to delivering on those promises, I've observed a different story. When I open a person's current portfolio, I can determine exactly what the previous advisor had in mind. It's obvious because of the high-commission, high-risk, and high-fee products. Far too many clients have simply done what they've been told to do by the "experts," thinking it was good and safe. But the truth is, oftentimes, it was neither. If the method to the madness of a financial plan isn't thoroughly explained and understood by the client, the client simply ends up with the madness part. And sometimes, it can take a year or two for me to unravel a current plan before I can begin laying a solid foundation.

I'm working with a single mom who is a nurse practitioner making $130,000 a year and is up to her eyeballs in debt. And deep down, I know I won't make a single penny from her. But that's okay. As my dad taught me through his paint jobs, sometimes you do a benevolent project simply because it's the right thing to do. And this gal needs a firm foundation before she can gain any real traction.

While I've touched on the importance of giving, there is another element you'll rarely hear financial advisors discuss—the aspect of **FORGIVENESS**. Many people have created such a mess with their finances that they don't know how to forgive themselves, and they find it difficult, if not impossible, to move forward. It's almost as if they are in a state of paralysis.

I once met a man who showed me his quarterly brokerage investment statement from a well-known, nationally-marketed financial firm. This was in April of 2009, during the Great Recession. In fourteen months, his assets had plunged from $1.3 million to $520,000—a 60% loss. He didn't know how he would ever tell his family, much less seek their forgiveness for some of the financial blunders he had made. He felt accountable for the mess he found himself in. He sat across from me in my office with his head buried in his hands, sobbing tears of regret uncontrollably, unable to even make eye contact with me. It was never his intention to lose money. He was trying to provide for his family, but unfortunately, he had bought into all the high-risk/high-return, flawed Wall Street formulas that provide a completely false sense of security. The worst part of the story is that he was sixty-two years old and totally oblivious to the high-risk stock position his broker had placed him in. He had built a house of cards with no foundation. When the storms came, the structure fell and created a total shambles.

But before we could dig him out of the rubble, he had to forgive himself first and then seek forgiveness from his wife and family. This was of paramount importance before moving forward because, at the core, that's how life really works. Real change is hard. It requires a change of heart and can be messy. But it's always worth it. When we are honest with ourselves and with our finances, it actually frees us. The same is true with forgiveness. Both are crucial for laying a foundation. Plus, doing the right thing the right way is not a bad philosophy to build on.

For close to four decades, I've been laying the groundwork with thousands of people, educating and helping them build comprehensive wealth plans, all while teaching them how money really works, which brings us back to the original question: "Why should you trust me?" I can only reply with a question of my own: "What more would anyone want in a financial advisor?"

Ultimately, if you want to understand how money works and build a solid foundation for a successful future, I can help. It begins with knowing what you want and why, the topic we'll discuss next.

KNOW WHAT YOU WANT & WHY

WHEN YOUR VALUES ARE CLEAR, YOUR DECISIONS ARE EASY.

—ROY DISNEY

I didn't begin adulthood with a clear game plan of what I wanted to do, but two things were certain: I wanted to be successful, and I didn't want to eke out a living. I had tasted success as a volley-ball player, and I knew what it was like to struggle with money. So, no matter what career path I chose, I wanted to be successful, so I wouldn't have to scramble my entire life to pay bills. In other words, I knew what I wanted and why.

This reminds me of the story of a man named Clay Anderson. Clay, like many youngsters who grew up in the sixties, dreamed of someday becoming an astronaut and traveling in space. This was, after all, the era when John Glenn, Buzz Aldrin, and Neil Armstrong were becoming American heroes.

As a young boy growing up in Nebraska, Clay's mother once covered him from head to toe with aluminum foil so he could participate in his hometown parade dressed as an astronaut. If only becoming an astronaut was that easy. But it's not.

NASA is extremely selective and accepts only a minuscule percentage of applicants, where the very top candidates are chosen. It's highly competitive and requires most astronaut-wannabes to obtain a master's degree in a relevant STEM field (science, technology, engineering, mathematics) and have at least two years of related work experience (or 1,000 hours of pilot-in-command flying time).

It took Clay fourteen years of applying before finally getting accepted into the NASA Space Program. From there, he underwent three years of rigorous training before eventually fulfilling his lifelong dream of traveling into space in 2007. That's when he became a member of the Expedition 15 crew and spent 152 days on board the International Space Station. Clay Anderson is truly a man who knows what he wants and why. Though many people drift their way through life, no one drifts their way into becoming an astronaut.

Likewise, you won't drift your way into becoming financially wealthy, either. It takes discipline. You don't want to get caught in the wrong current. If you're not 100% sure about what you want in life, don't despair. You are not alone. You picked up this book for a reason, and I bet it's because you wanted to gain a better understanding of money and wealth. With regard to finances, let me encourage you to begin by defining and shaping exactly what you want to accomplish.

DEFINING RETIREMENT

Typically, when it comes to financial planning, the focus is on retirement. Yet when I ask people to define retirement, their answers are all over the map. Some people want to have enough money to travel the world. Others want to play golf every week or lie in a hammock sipping adult beverages all day long. Others want to start a nonprofit or have the ability to spoil their grandkids. If we're honest, many people simply don't want to run out of money and spend their final years alone and/or broke. From my financial perspective, perhaps the best definition of retirement is simply,

"To be able to do what you want to do when you want to do it."

Your path to true wealth begins by clarifying your values and your *why*. You'll never hit the mark if you don't have a target. A vague hope of having enough money when you stop working is just that—a vague hope. Hope is not a financial strategy. It's time to get crystal clear and plan your life more intentionally.

Did you know that numerous studies have shown that most self-made, financially wealthy people have five similar life habits in common? And ironically, none of them have to do with investment strategies or working harder. Statistically speaking, the majority of self-made millionaires follow habits such as:

❶ They rise early.

❷ They exercise regularly.

❸ They eat healthy.

"DEFINITION OF RETIREMENT: TO BE ABLE TO **DO WHAT YOU WANT** TO DO **WHEN YOU WANT** TO DO **IT**."

–PHIL BODINE

❹ They read books.

❺ They watch little or no TV.

This is not an exclusive list, nor is it exhaustive. It's simply a fascinating way to demonstrate that creating true wealth requires discipline and intentionality.

While I'm not here to discuss your eating, sleeping, or exercise routines, I do want to help you define a standard for your financial success so we can begin to lay the groundwork for whatever financial desires you have in mind. Acquiring true wealth also requires an abundance mindset rather than one of scarcity.

SCARCITY MINDSET	VS	ABUNDANCE THINKING
With a *scarcity mindset*, one:		On the other hand, *abundance thinking*:
… fears change;		… takes ownership of change;
… thinks small and avoids risk;		… thinks big and embraces risk;
… believes times are tough;		… believes the best is yet to come;
… resents competition;		… strives to grow;
… is suspicious of others;		… welcomes competition;
… won't offer help to others;		… trusts and builds rapport with others;
… won't share knowledge;		… freely offers help to others;
… **focuses on the payment**;		… **focuses on the price**;
… hoards things;		… is generous with others;
… believes there will never be enough.		… believes there will always be more!

Once you begin shifting your thinking from scarcity to abundance, you can incorporate some of the foundational strategies toward building a healthy financial future.

9 CORE PRINCIPLES FOR FINANCIAL TRANSFORMATION

Whenever I work with a new client, my job is to help them set sustainable goals and maintain forward progress in meeting those goals. When it comes to setting financial goals and objectives, I believe there are **NINE CORE PRINCIPLES** (building blocks) that make up a great foundation to help you. This is what I believe separates our work from all other advisors. See if you agree.

❶ Optimize your full wealth potential and create the highest efficiency on every dollar at work while creating a quality of life that exceeds your expectations.

❷ Have the **RIGHT** to spend, give, and enjoy your wealth without the fear of running out.

❸ Pass your wealth on to your family or charity . . . **NOT** other wealthy people by way of an estate sale, financial institutions, or the IRS. Remember, it's Your$, not The**IRS**.

❹ Recapture **lost opportunity costs** or monies currently leaking from your overall assets, unknowingly.

❺ Have no additional out-of-pocket costs relative to your current plan to give you more wealth vs. take wealth from you.

❻ Take no additional risk relative to the current plan (strategy-based … **<u>NOT</u>** product-based).

❼ Pay no additional taxes, or preferably fewer taxes.

❽ The plan <u>**must work under all circumstances**</u> (tax increases, inflation, recession, stock market decline, lawsuits, death, becoming disabled, etc.) where you hope for the best and prepare for the worst.

❾ Create a plan that provides **Peace of Mind**— socially, emotionally, spiritually, and financially.

Sounds pretty good, doesn't it?

Now let me ask you this:

How does your current financial plan line up with the principles above?

Please understand that this list is more like a standard to help you make financial decisions based on criteria instead of simply buying products and hoping they produce.

Anyone can shovel their money into a 401(k) and see what happens. A better approach is to have a clear understanding of who you are and what you value.

The goal of this book isn't to turn you into a billionaire or even an astronaut. It's to help you understand what it takes to be able to do what you want to do when you want to do it. And quite frankly, financially healthy people think and do things differently than those drifting through life with vague hopes.

I want you to really think about what you want and what you are doing. I challenge you to define your target, dig deep, and figure out why it's important to you. It's worth repeating these nine principles will help you shift into a higher financial gear, so take a look at them again.

9 CORE PRINCIPLES FOR FINANCIAL TRANSFORMATION

① Optimize your full wealth potential and create the highest efficiency on every dollar to create a quality of life that exceeds your expectations.

② Have the **RIGHT** to spend, give, and enjoy your wealth without fear of running out.

③ Pass your wealth to your family or charity … **NOT** other wealthy people. It's Your$, not The**IRS**.

④ Recapture **lost opportunity costs** or monies leaking from your overall assets, unknowingly.

⑤ Have no additional out-of-pocket costs relative to your current plan to give you more wealth vs. take wealth from you.

⑥ Take no additional risk relative to the current plan (strategy-based … **NOT** product-based).

⑦ Pay no additional taxes, preferably fewer taxes.

⑧ The plan **must work under all circumstances** where you hope for the best and prepare for the worst.

⑨ Create a plan that provides **PEACE OF MIND**: socially, emotionally, spiritually, and financially.

Most people go through life spending very little time on introspection. Why not take a few minutes right now to ask yourself the following questions? Think them through honestly, and if you're really bold, record your answers.

WHAT DO YOU WANT & WHY WORKSHEET

What are your three most important financial objectives, in order of importance?

1)

2)

3)

Who do you rely on for financial advice?

What's important to you about money?

If there's **one** thing you could work on that would dramatically improve your life, what would it be?

_____

_____

_____

What is most sacred to you?

_____

_____

_____

What's something really important to you that you rarely get a chance to talk about?

_____

_____

_____

What do you like to do when you're not working?

_____

_____

_____

If someone gave you a million dollars, what would you do with it?

If money were no issue, what would you do with your life?

What's the most dramatic thing you now know about money that was not possible to know from your upbringing?

What are the consequences if you don't have a financial plan?

What's the #1 thing you want to be remembered for by your family?

_____

_____

_____

If you can formulate a goal with a clear understanding of what you want and *why* it's important to you, you'll be on your way to what I like to call "values-based planning." It's a much richer and more meaningful way to approach life than simply hoping your dreams come true.

A goal without a plan is simply a wish.

—Antoine de Saint-Exupéry

But a goal with a plan backed with values gives you a sense of purpose and makes decision-making much easier. Your mind transitions from one of hope … to one of belief.

Keep in mind that many financial planners in today's world are transaction-driven and not necessarily relationship-oriented. Advisors, accountants, and attorneys generally feel most at ease when they are talking about numbers. Many will shy away from questions involving philosophical or emotional answers because it's too time-consuming and requires more mental energy. Plus, it's outside of their comfort zone. Why do you think lawyers often want to draw up the shortest wills and the smallest trusts imaginable? Because they want to turn them into mundane, boilerplate transactions. They feel there's no need to get caught up in all the family details. They'd rather just keep things simple. "Here's your trust, here's your will, here's my card, and here's your bill."

Recently, a woman stopped into my office and asked me to look at her portfolio. She told me she didn't trust her current advisor, and she had no idea what was actually in her plan. After handing me a two-inch thick binder with her latest monthly statement, she asked me for my feedback. I told her we could do a forensic audit and look over the entire landscape, but first, I wanted to know what she was looking for in a financial advisor. And I wanted to know what was most important to her in life.

This led to a lengthy discussion about work and family, where I discovered that she had a high aversion to risk and a desire to take a more conservative approach to her investing. After studying her plan, it became obvious why she was confused and frustrated. The risk in her portfolio was out of touch with her values. It was completely out of alignment. No wonder she didn't trust her advisor.

Life is more than numbers and formulas. That's why I place a high degree of importance on understanding values, emotions, and intentions.

Typical financial planning doesn't necessarily provide the best answers, especially when life doesn't go according to plan, so knowing your why is important. It provides a sense of purpose that drives you toward the future you really want. And if your advisor actually understands what interests you, engages you, and motivates you, he'll have a much better chance at helping you achieve your dreams.

The woman I mentioned became my client, and we totally revamped her investments in a way that made sense to her and was much more aligned with how she operates. In short, we did a little values-based planning.

It might be surprising to hear this, but in my experience, most people don't have a money problem. They have a mindset problem. They've never fully processed who they are, what they want, and why it's important to them. In other words, they've never really connected with their core values. They don't know their *why*.

The sooner you can grasp *why* certain things are important to you and *why* you value them, the easier it will be to lay solid groundwork to propel you forward. This step is paramount. You can no longer just hope and see what happens. If you're going to shoot for the moon, you have to set a course and put it in motion, just like an astronaut. Because, quite frankly, you'll never get there by drifting.

Peak Performance Tip #1

What is your **WHY**, and does your current plan support it?
Knowing **WHAT** you want and **WHY** will help you **LAY A SOLID FOUNDATION**
for your financial plan and **PROPEL YOU** toward your dreams.

DON'T ROCK THE BOAT

THE IDEA THAT I SHOULD TRUST MY EYES
MORE THAN THE STATS, I DON'T BUY THAT
BECAUSE I'VE SEEN MAGICIANS PULL
RABBITS OUT OF HATS AND I KNOW
THAT THE RABBIT'S NOT IN THERE.

—BILLY BEANE

I'll never forget my time at that small financial planning firm when I began my career. While I did receive some training, most of it was based on a company philosophy that went something like this: "Just do what everyone else is doing, and you'll be fine." Unfortunately, that only works if you're surrounded by superstars, and like most of the working world, I was not. I had to think differently if I wanted a win-win for my clients and myself. This reminds me of one of my favorite sports stories . . .

In the fall of 2001, the Oakland A's professional baseball team lost three of its star players to richer teams via free agency and was once again thrust into a mode of trying to rebuild their team with one of the smallest budgets in the sport. As General Manager Billy Beane stated in the movie *Moneyball*, "The problem we're trying to solve is that there are rich teams and there are poor teams. Then there's fifty feet of crap. And then there's us."[1]

Frustrated by the system, Beane courageously challenged conventional wisdom by assembling a roster of players largely overlooked by the old guard of coaches, scouts, general managers, and owners. His theory was that the typical system was flawed. He bet against a century of history by hiring bargain-bin players based on key undervalued performance metrics instead of on appearance, over-hyped stats, and personality.

Both the concept and team seemed foolhardy at first, as fans and journalists mocked the audacity of someone trying to buck the system. However, in the end, Billy Beane not only assembled the biggest bargain team in baseball, he turned the sports world on its head by calling into question everything the experts thought they knew about the game. And in the process, he completely revolutionized how the sport is conducted today!

Similarly, we live in a culture of century-old financial systems designed to keep us following the crowd but not necessarily bring us wealth. In other words, **we are taught WHAT to think, but not HOW to think.**

It takes courage to question where the crowd is heading and begin making decisions based on what really works versus conventional wisdom. Now, I'm not saying you need to be radical or try to revolutionize history. But what I am saying is that perhaps it's time to take a closer look at what most people are doing and why they are doing it. And then maybe you'll discover a smarter, more efficient way of getting where you want to go than simply following the crowd.

THE "POT ROAST PRINCIPLE"

When it comes to investing, many people follow what I like to call "The Pot Roast Principle." Maybe you're familiar with this story.

One day, a young girl noticed her mother cutting the ends off a pot roast before putting it into the oven. She had seen her mom do this many times before, but for the first time, she decided to ask why.

Her mom replied, "I'm not sure why I cut the ends off. It's something my mother always did, so I do it, too. Why don't you ask your grandmother?"

Intrigued, the young girl called her grandmother and asked, "Grandma, why do you cut the ends off of the pot roast before you cook it?"

Her grandmother replied, "You know, I'm not sure. That's just the way my mother always cooked it. Why don't you ask her?"

Determined to find an answer, the young girl called her great-grandmother and asked, "Back when you used to fix family meals, why did you cut the ends off of the pot roast before cooking it?

To the young girl's amazement, her great-grandmother responded, "When I was first married, we had a very small oven, and the pot roast didn't fit inside unless I cut the ends off."

Just doing something because it's what everyone else has done doesn't necessarily make it a good idea. How many "pot roast traditions" are you blindly following in your life? When we don't ask questions, we end up making assumptions. And in the financial world, that can be costly. Ignorance is not bliss when it comes to money.

ROCKING THE BOAT

There's nothing wrong with staying the course on a steady ship . . . as long as it's heading in the right direction. If not, it may be time to rock the boat.

Sticking with the status quo is no way to get ahead. People who follow sheep get no further than the herd. And since most people are not financially wealthy, your odds of success are not good if you stay on such a path.

I find that many people not only suffer from a lack of knowledge, but in most cases, they don't even know what they don't know. As a result, they struggle to get ahead.

Recently, I was interviewed for a nationally publicized financial planning magazine. The interviewer asked me the question, "Given all your years of experience, what are the most common unintended financial mistakes you see people make?" I came up with eight of them immediately, and they are almost always part of "following the crowd." Let's take a look.

THE 8 MOST COMMON UNINTENDED FINANCIAL MISTAKES

MISTAKE #1: What they want and what they have are totally different.

Most people want more freedom, flexibility, and control, with less risk and greater returns, but sometimes the gap is too wide to make their wishes come true. They want investments that provide more time with family, the ability to travel, and maybe even a second home. Surprisingly, many people think they already have a plan like that in place. They bought it from a friend of a friend who works as a financial planner. However, once I look at their portfolio, I see a completely different picture.

The freedom, flexibility, and control they desire are trapped inside a plan that will keep their money locked away for years if not decades. The small risk and great returns they envisioned are stagnant investments that just inch along, waiting for the next market crash or pandemic to level them out.

MISTAKE #2: They are unaware of their present financial position.

Every home has a supply drawer filled with scissors, rubber bands, batteries, paper, pens, etc. But if yours is like mine, it also serves as the junk drawer, where miscellaneous items like charging cords, grocery coupons, gas receipts, and mail flyers get added to the mix. This can be frustrating when I'm in need of something simple like a paper clip or a thumbtack, and the cluttered mess turns my simple search into an hour-long treasure hunt. Does this sound familiar?

This is the same way many people treat their finances. For starters, they don't know their assets. Most people don't have a well-structured financial plan; they have a drawer full of statements. We call it the **"FINANCIAL JUNK DRAWER MENTALITY."** They have a box or a file cabinet that contains things like old life insurance policies purchased years ago from the credit union. Or, it may include shares of stock that were acquired on a whim because of an inside tip from a trusted co-worker. There's probably a folder with 401(k) statements and perhaps even a savings bond or a mortgage contract in the pile. The file box is filled with all kinds of miscellaneous documents, papers, and receipts. But really, it's just a financial junk drawer. There is no rhyme or reason, strategy or structure. It's just a hodgepodge of fragmented, mentally unorganized financial stuff. Trying to find the right document at the right time is like trying to find the proverbial needle in a haystack. Does this sound equally familiar?

PLANNING WITHOUT A ROADMAP
The Financial Junk Drawer Mentality

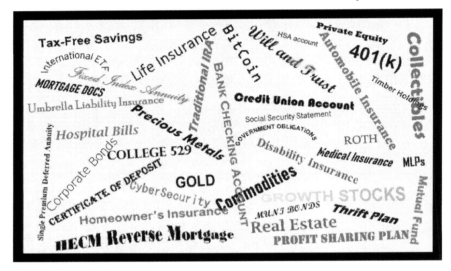

Not only are many people unaware of their assets, but even more don't know their debts. Years ago, I took on a married couple as new clients. She was a former banker, and he was a urologist making about $900,000 a year. Yet they lamented that they had no money, which perplexed me.

After our initial meeting, I felt I wasn't getting the full story. So, I scheduled our next meeting to take place at their home. I wanted to get a better lay of the land and see exactly what I was dealing with.

As I drove up, I noticed three European luxury cars in the driveway. In addition, there was an RV, a speedboat, and a bass boat. I probed deeper into their spending habits, and the first thing

I discovered was that their daily routine consisted of eating out nearly every night (and it wasn't fast food). They were also prone to embarking on jet-setting jaunts across the world to all kinds of lavish vacation destinations.

It was a classic case of style over substance. They were what I like to refer to as "financial alcoholics." A more polite way of putting it would be, "Big hat, no cattle." They were simply on a consumption treadmill with no plan to get off.

One of the problems that arises with having an enormous income is that it can bring about an invincible feeling that the money will never run out. As a result, it's easy to get lazy with tracking expenses. But continually living for the here and now is no way to prepare for long-term wealth, plus accruing debt will only pull you backward. Eventually, you have to pay the piper.

This scenario is way more common than you'd ever want to imagine. Throughout my career, I've spent time with multiple business owners of large and small companies who preach to their executive teams about budgets and cash flow. Yet, individually, they have no idea where they stand with their own personal finances.

There is a huge difference between **THINKING** you know your monthly expenses and **KNOWING** them. If you don't stay on top of what you spend, you will get nickeled-and-dimed to death. It is critical to know how much you spend and what you spend it on if you want to gain control of your financial future. Yet many people are clueless in this area. My advice is that you should track all of your expenses and then stop spending money you don't have on things you can't afford just to try to impress people you don't even like.

MISTAKE #3: They lack a financial plan or road map.

Most people don't know what they don't know, and what they do know can be downright scary. With so many products, plans, and "experts" banging on their doors every day, it's hard to know what to believe.

A recent study from Red Crow Marketing found that the average person will view between 4,000 and 10,000 advertisements every single day![2] They don't lack information; they lack *complete* information. And partial information partnered with a selfish desire to get ahead quickly can lead to all kinds of foolish financial faux pas.

It's critical to have a road map for where you want to go financially, but you have to follow one that is accurate and heading in the right direction. Could you imagine building a house without a blueprint? What about a castle?

Rather than having a financial plan that resembles the junk drawer above, where everything is chaotic and hodge-podge, instead, I want you to consider a plan that is strategic, ordered, and has a purpose. By analogy, what if your financial plan is like a castle made up of all kinds of financial tools that offer protection, savings, and growth?

In medieval times, kings and lords would build a moat around their castle to protect them from unwelcome invading forces.

Today, we have our own castles (personal wealth), but we no longer have moats to protect our life savings from unwelcome wealth-eroding forces (market drops, taxes, health problems, unforeseen life events, etc.).

"WHEN A PERSON DOES NOT **KNOW** WHICH HARBOR THEY ARE HEADED FOR, NO WIND IS **THE RIGHT WIND**."

—LUCIUS ANNAEUS SENECA

Consider your financial plan as a castle made up of all kinds of financial tools ranging from savings accounts to real estate to 401(k)s and stocks/bonds. Take a look at the castle on the opposite page and write down or circle the financial tools you are currently using. Are you employing lots of tools, a few tools, or barely any?

By implementing defensive strategies into your financial life, you will have created a modern-day moat to help better insulate your wealth. When you incorporate protection, savings, and growth options, ranging from cash accounts, insurance plans, real estate, retirement plans, and investments, you are on your way to achieving order and financial structure.

YOUR FINANCIAL CASTLE

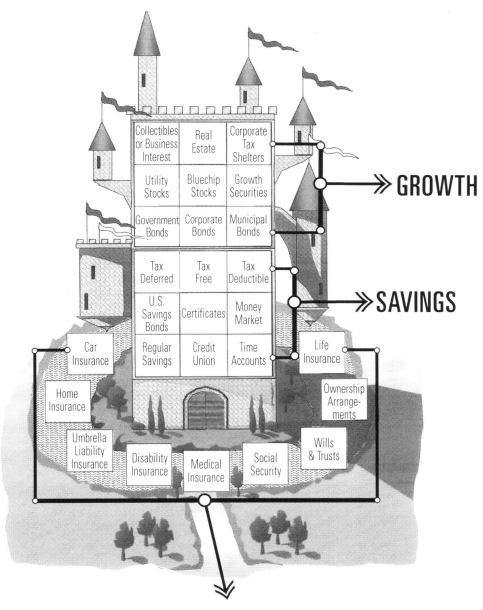

GROWTH

Collectibles or Business Interest	Real Estate	Corporate Tax Shelters
Utility Stocks	Bluechip Stocks	Growth Securities
Government Bonds	Corporate Bonds	Municipal Bonds

SAVINGS

Tax Deferred	Tax Free	Tax Deductible
U.S. Savings Bonds	Certificates	Money Market
Regular Savings	Credit Union	Time Accounts

Car Insurance

Home Insurance

Umbrella Liability Insurance

Disability Insurance

Medical Insurance

Social Security

Life Insurance

Ownership Arrangements

Wills & Trusts

FOUNDATION OF PROTECTION

The key is to have a financial plan using some variation of the tools so it will hold up under turbulent conditions. You don't want to put all your eggs in one basket—it needs to vary, what is called diversification. Any healthy financial plan needs to have these **NINE IMPORTANT COMPONENTS:**

❶ A systematic flow of money into the plan.

❷ A good return on that money.

❸ Easy access to that money.

❹ Minimum or no taxes on the growth of that money.

❺ Paying the lowest tax possible on withdrawal from the plan.

❻ Easy distribution of the money.

❼ Contingencies for emergency needs.

❽ Minimal potential loss.

❾ Flexibility to change the plan.

MISTAKE #4: They're not saving and investing enough money.

The difference between the haves and the have-nots is **DISCIPLINE.** Most people **give up long-term financial success for short-term "cool,"** meaning they spend more than they make to impress other people. They will sacrifice for what they want most for what they want **NOW.** And **NOW** is the most expensive word in the English language. I see this, especially among young adults. It has always been a sad fact that the great American consumer is so accustomed to taking their money or savings to go out and buy more stuff when they could be using it to buy independence and autonomy.

**Steady plodding leads to prosperity,
hasty speculation leads to poverty.**

—Proverbs 21:5 (TLB)

Since this book revolves around *Wealth in Overdrive®*, most Americans are not adding enough fuel to their engine to get from point A to point B (i.e., they're not saving or investing enough). For example, driving from my office in Sacramento, CA, to my office in Fort Wayne, IN, would require me to refuel my car multiple times to get to my destination. The average savings rate of the average American is 3.8%,[3] but we recommend saving a minimum of 15% to 20% of gross income.

In general, I've found that most people handle their money in one of two ways:

The Debtors (PAYING INTEREST METHOD):

The first way involves people who live lives that revolve around borrowing and paying back, borrowing and paying back, borrowing and paying back. This is the "Paying Interest Method," and it's how most Americans operate. The life of a **Debtor** resembles this chart:

THE DEBTOR

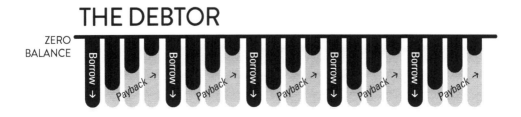

"MOST **GIVE UP** LONG-TERM WEALTH FOR **SHORT-TERM** **'COOL'** TO IMPRESS PEOPLE."

–PHIL BODINE

"POOR PEOPLE BUY THINGS. RICH PEOPLE **BUY ASSETS** THAT **PRODUCE CASH FLOW**."

–ROBERT KIYOSAKI,
RICH DAD POOR DAD

The Savers (LOSING INTEREST METHOD):

The second group of people live their lives that rotate the other way. They save their money, which is good, and then they spend it; save, then spend; save, then spend. And they pay cash. While they save on interest payments, they lose the benefit of the interest they would have earned on those dollars for the rest of their lives. This is also known as the "Losing Interest Method." The life of the **Saver** looks like this:

The truth is, it doesn't matter which approach people take; they always end up back at ground zero. Banks love both types of people, and neither method provides any real long-term gain.

There's actually a lesser-known third group of people:

The Wealth Optimizers (WEALTH IN OVERDRIVE® METHOD):

Similar to the Saver, Wealth Optimizers save in steps. However, if they need to spend money, they borrow funds against their saved money as collateral. Like using a car as collateral on a loan, they don't lose ownership of their car. And in this case, they don't lose ownership of their money, either. It's as if it never leaves their account. As a result, it continues to earn **uninterrupted compounded interest** while they pay back the loan with amortized interest credited back to their account. The **Wealth in Overdrive® method** allows them to save and spend their money at the same time without losing interest and without interrupting the growth of the exponential wealth curve.

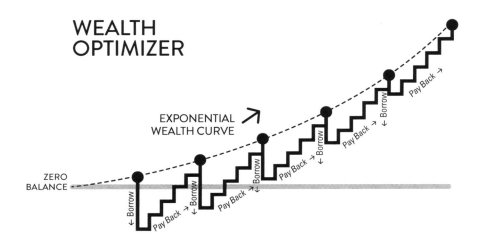

WEALTH OPTIMIZER

EXPONENTIAL WEALTH CURVE

ZERO BALANCE

> **THE MIRACLE OF UNINTERRUPTED COMPOUNDED WEALTH IS THE SECRET TO GETTING YOUR MONEY OUT WITHOUT LOSING ITS EARNINGS POTENTIAL.**

MISTAKE #5: They're white-collar individuals making blue-collar financial decisions.

If you'll remember, I was raised in a blue-collar working household with a stay-at-home mom in the cornfields of Indiana, and I've found that the majority of people in the blue-collar working world like to follow a simple two-step investment strategy that consists of throwing money into their 401(k) and trying to pay down their mortgage.

Surprisingly, this is somewhat common with white-collar workers, as well. While the process is sincere and somewhat admirable, it's a poor way to generate wealth. It's like driving down the highway with one foot on the gas pedal and the other on the brake. On the one hand (foot), you are investing. But on the other, you're handcuffing yourself to an inflexible vehicle that watches your investment get eaten alive by taxes.

As your income rises, your financial strategies need to change. You'll never develop true white-collar wealth with a blue-collar investment mentality.

MISTAKE #6: They unknowingly pay more taxes than they should.

No one enjoys paying taxes—that's a given. The problem is most people don't understand how to incorporate tax strategies into their financial planning. As a result, they pay way too much to the IRS.

THE HARD TRUTH IS THAT MOST AMERICANS WILL PAY MORE IN TAXES THAN THEY WILL EVER SAVE OR INVEST FOR RETIREMENT. IN THE END, TAXES END UP BECOMING THEIR BIGGEST EXPENSE.

—Phil Bodine

If there are ways to legally lower the taxes you pay or allow you to utilize your tax spending as a financial advantage, wouldn't you want to know about it? It makes me think about this quote from Grant Cordone, the CEO of Cardone Capital:

> So let me get this straight . . . I'm paying TAXES on my wages, then paying SALES TAX to spend my own money, then paying INCOME TAX on money that was ALREADY TAXED, then when I die, my kids pay the DEATH TAX on my money that was ALREADY TAXED? And then people HATE me for doing everything I can TO REDUCE my TAXES?[4]

Keep in mind that lowering your tax bill by structuring your transactions to reap tax benefits is not only legal, it's extremely wise. Tax evasion, however (deceit, subterfuge, or concealment), is a crime.

Paraphrasing a quote often attributed to U.S. District Trial Judge Learned Hand, **"There are two tax systems in America: one for the informed, and one for the uninformed. Both are legal."**

Unfortunately, in my professional experience, I've found that most people fall into the "uninformed" category.

MISTAKE #7: They are unaware of their risk exposure.

So many people have bought into the flawed Wall Street formula and philosophy that **more risk equals more reward**. But that has never worked.

I truly believe that no one has ever really read a prospectus. If they actually did, they would never invest their money (trust me, just reading the first two pages will convince you). In fact, the only guarantee I ever make to my clients is that if they play the stock market, they will lose money at some point. As Mark Twain once said, "There are two times in a man's life when he should not speculate: when he can't afford it, and when he can."[5]

I like to ask my clients to think about: **"How much *more* money would you have today if you simply avoided the unnecessary risks you shouldn't have taken in the past?"**

Then, I like to show them a graph of someone whose investments are getting a steady 6% to 7% return versus someone whose investments continually fluctuate between a 28% return and a 10% loss. It's a substantial difference. Unfortunately, there's something so alluring about the prospect of "hitting it big" that overly

Judge Billings Learned Hand
U.S. Court of Appeals (1924–1951)

"THERE ARE TWO TAX SYSTEMS IN AMERICA: ONE FOR THE **INFORMED,** AND ONE FOR THE **UNINFORMED. BOTH ARE LEGAL**."

JUDGE LEARNED HAND

ambitious investors are willing to throw caution to the wind and rationalize their losses. Addicted gamblers do the same thing. In the end, it's a terrible way to build true wealth.

I have a client who is a CPA. His wife was a health administrator. When she left her job at the hospital, she had accrued $380,000 in assets, which she agreed to let her husband manage since he was, after all, a CPA.

When they showed me their account, I was astounded at the amount of risk they were taking. There were red flags all over the place. I told the husband, "Look, if you want to buy into this risk thing, that's up to you. But you're just out there guessing. It really all comes down to this: How much more money would you have today if you hadn't taken all the unnecessary risks up to this point?"

His wife stood up and applauded.

MISTAKE #8: They procrastinate.

The world is full of procrastinators. In the world of finance, waiting even a couple of years to get your finances in order can cost you thousands. Unfortunately, I meet people every day who simply "want to think about it." I guess the old adage about leading a horse to water is true. Ultimately, it's up to the client to put the ball in motion.

If there's one thing I've learned in nearly forty years of dealing with people, it's this: *no one likes to lose money.* It doesn't matter how old you are. It doesn't matter how much money you have in your account.

Consistent, solid investment strategies are a much better way to acquire true wealth. I want to challenge you . . . would you ever

"HOW MUCH MORE MONEY WOULD YOU HAVE **TODAY** IF YOU SIMPLY **AVOIDED THE UNNECESSARY RISKS** YOU SHOULDN'T HAVE TAKEN **IN THE PAST?**"

–PHIL BODINE

intentionally and consciously make a decision to lose money? Just remember this: **the price of discipline is always less than the pain of regret.**

In the end, not rocking the boat is a great way to experience a lifetime of mediocrity.

HOW TO AVOID THE 8 MOST COMMON UNINTENDED MISTAKES

THE MISTAKES MOST PEOPLE MAKE	WHAT WE RECOMMEND INSTEAD
1. What they want and what they have are totally different.	1. Make certain your financial plan is in alignment with your values.
2. They are unaware of their present financial position.	2. Take the time to gather and organize all of your financial information and inventory into one place to gain more clarity on your current financial position. Communicate this to your loved ones.
3. They lack a financial plan or roadmap.	3. Create a game plan and/or dashboard with your financial advisor to better chart your course.
4. They are not saving and investing enough money.	4. Make certain you are putting enough fuel into your engine—a minimum of 15% of your gross income.
5. They are white-collar individuals making blue-collar financial decisions.	5. Beware of the status quo. Conventional wisdom is not always correct.
6. They unknowingly pay more taxes than they should.	6. Redeploy your assets away from tax deferral and implement strategies that limit taxation.
7. They are unaware of their risk exposure.	7. Employ financial strategies that take less risk and create more benefits.
8. They procrastinate.	8. Don't wait. Initiate your financial game plan as soon as possible.

Peak Performance Tip #2

DON'T MISS THIS!

The miracle of **UNINTERRUPTED COMPOUNDED WEALTH**
is the **SECRET** to accessing your money
without losing its **EARNINGS POTENTIAL**.

THREE

UNDERSTANDING THE BASICS

GENTLEMEN, THIS IS A FOOTBALL.
—VINCE LOMBARDI

Do you remember the first time you received a piece of mail from a bank inviting you to open an account or a credit card?

I do. I was a freshman in college, and I was excited. After all, banks create quite an impression on young people. They offer free lollipops, air conditioning, and really cool bank vaults. What's not to like? There are armored guards and personnel dressed in fancy clothing wearing friendly smiles. The building itself is made of granite and has a gorgeous landscape with fountains. There's even a sign out in front that displays the time and temperature. How can anyone not like banks?

Chances are high that even your parents were excited when they helped you open your first account. It's a big moment. I mean, you couldn't keep all that birthday money stashed under your bed forever, could you?

And since that day, just like with me, you've probably never stopped receiving a continual stream of ads reinforcing the culturally accepted message that banks should be the primary holding tank for all of your money.

This scenario plays out day after day all across our country. It's part of Americana. Who would dare question such a nostalgic rite of passage in our young financial lives?

Not to be a party pooper, but here's a little news flash: Banks ARE businesses, and they are in business to make a profit! If they don't, they close their doors and go out of business.

I know of no other business that reaps the benefit of such culturally conditioned, follow-the-rule consumers as banks. It's rarely even questioned. That's just what we do in our country. We go to banks. End of story. We should all be so lucky as to run our own bank.

Once you understand how financial institutions operate, you'll see that I'm not joking. If we all ran our finances like bank owners, we'd be doing quite well. And that's exactly what I'm about to share with you–the *HOW*.

THE FOUR GOLDEN RULES OF ALL FINANCIAL INSTITUTIONS

There are four basic rules that all financial institutions operate by. When I refer to financial institutions, I'm talking about banks, insurance companies, credit unions, wirehouses, Wall Street, and lending companies. When you understand these rules, you will begin to see things in a whole new light.

RULE #1: They want ALL of your money. (PROFIT)

Not just part of it. They want to control all of it. All the time. They want to make a profit. Banks, credit unions, insurance companies, money management firms, and even the IRS don't manufacture anything. They just trade money. So they need it, and the more, the merrier.

Which means they need you. So, they lure you in with shiny incentives. For example, they might offer you a free fleece blanket or an umbrella with your favorite sports team logo if you open an account. Or perhaps they'll give you free checking if you sign up "today." The key is to get the ball rolling.

Believe it or not, years ago, banks offered a free toaster to any family who opened a new account. Can you imagine providing a link to all your finances for the mere price of a toaster? Sounds crazy, but it worked—and it still does today.

RULE #2: They want your money on a regular, ongoing, systematic basis. (CASHFLOW)

I'm sure you've heard the saying, "He laughed all the way to the bank," meaning he made a great deal of money very easily. This is often used as the punchline of a joke. But now, it's the banks who are laughing. They don't have to go anywhere. The money comes straight to them, and it's never been easier.

As you know, physical paychecks are a thing of the past. Paydays consist of transactions where money is automatically deposited directly into an individual's bank account. Your bank sees your money before you do.

What an incredible deal it must be to have a system that automatically streams revenue straight into your business on a regular, ongoing basis. It's so seamless that customers don't have to think about it. And, it's often more of a hassle for a customer to stop the auto payments than to start them.

I have to believe that if a genie popped out of a lamp and granted me three wishes, this automated system would be one of them. It doesn't get any better than regular, ongoing, automated deposits. It's what every smart business owner would want, and amazingly, it's what every financial institution in the country now has.

RULE #3: They want to hold onto your money for as long as possible, forever if they can. (LONGEVITY)

Let me ask you a question. If you were the bank, how long would you want to have control over the money being deposited? As long as humanly possible, right? Every account that closes is considered lost revenue. Thus, the goal is to control a customer's money forever.

As a result, financial institutions come up with all kinds of clever, unassuming ways to keep your money locked up. How? CDs, IRAs, 401(k)s, early withdrawal penalties, dividend reinvestment, capital gains reinvestment, and trust departments. And, of course, there's the always-promoted "miracle" of compound interest.

The truth is, these are simply instruments designed to keep your money in the financial institution for a really long time. It's like putting your money in jail. You lose liquidity, use, and control. If you want to take it out early, you get penalized. It's locked up so nice and tight that you have to jump through hoops to gain access. These programs are designed that way for a reason.

RULE #4: They want to give as little money back to you as possible. (LEVERAGE)

In physics, you can achieve more with a lever than without it. The same can be applied to math. Banks have mastered the art of financial leverage by using their customers' money to gain a higher return than would be possible using their own assets. They do this by leveraging the money deposited by one customer, then turning it around and lending it to another.

For example, Customer A deposits $100 into his account, and the bank pays him 1% for the use of that money. The bank's liability is $100 plus the 1% interest they pay that customer = $101 in total. Banks are not charities. For them to stay in business, they need to lend that $100 out to Customer B at a rate higher than 1%. For this example, let's say Customer B needs to obtain a loan and is charged 4% by the bank. After the bank pays off its liability of $101 to Customer A and gets back $104 from Customer B, it ends up with a $3 profit. This may seem like a small figure, but remember, banks have perfected the art of getting their customers' money to flow through them at an inferior rate before passing it on at a superior rate.

The bank spent $1 to earn $4. That small profit of $3 is actually a 300% Return on Investment (ROI). Imagine how these little profits are harvested daily on the billions of dollars that run through banks. It all adds up. That's leverage, and it's powerful! The key is to understand this principle so that you can get it to work for you in your own personal tax-free banking strategy.

HOW BANKS LEVERAGE YOUR MONEY

ENTITY	INVESTMENT	PROFIT	BANK'S ROI
CUSTOMER A DEPOSIT	$100	-$1	-1%
BANK LOAN TO CUSTOMER B	$100	$4	4%
BANK	$1	$3	300%

Are you following this? You give them your money and receive 1% interest. They give you their money, and you have to pay them 4%. What's wrong with this picture?

It doesn't take a genius to see which side is getting the better deal. It's always to the bank's advantage to collect and loan out as much money as possible. In essence, a bank can make up to twenty-four separate loans on every dollar it collects, whether in the form of a deposit or a loan repayment.

Let's say the bank lends you money to buy a car, and they charge you 6% interest on that loan. When you make your car payment, those same dollars go back into the bank.

Then, the bank loans those exact same dollars back out to you or someone else again, only this time, it's in the form of a credit card. You then make your credit card payment with 18% interest, and the same money goes back to the bank.

If the bank gives you a home mortgage at 7% and you make your house payment, where does your money go? Right! It goes

"DO WHAT
THE BANKS DO,
NOT WHAT
THEY TELL YOU
TO DO. THEY
ARE TEACHING
YOU **WHAT**
TO THINK
NOT **HOW TO
THINK**."

—PHIL BODINE

straight back to the bank, ready to be loaned out yet again, this time in the form of a boat loan at 9%.

Are you getting the picture? You're paying the bank an awful lot to transfer your money back and forth.

VELOCITY OF MONEY MULTIPLIER

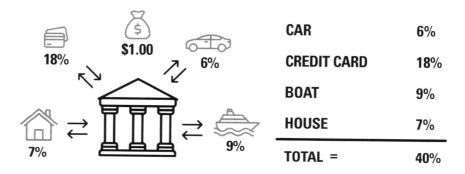

CAR	6%
CREDIT CARD	18%
BOAT	9%
HOUSE	7%
TOTAL =	40%

I hope you're starting to see a pattern. All financial institutions operate with these four objectives, and most people never question any of it. However, to get ahead financially, it's paramount to understand how this works and realize there has to be a better way than simply helping the banks get rich off of your hard-earned money. The above examples represent **THEIR** system where **THEY** benefit the most. Somehow, we have been told the above is a good idea. Typical advice says we position our assets in a way that is better for the institutions.

Remember, money must remain in motion, or it becomes stagnant. That's why banks consider money in their vault a liability, not an asset.

WE ARE ASKING THE WRONG QUESTIONS

One of the most basic objectives should be to ask good questions. Unfortunately, most people are asking the wrong questions. If you Google the topic "Most Commonly Asked Financial Questions," here's a sample of what you'll find:

"How do I save more money?"
"How do I improve my credit score?"
"How much do I need to save for retirement?"
"How do I choose a bank for my savings account?"
"Are online banks safe?"
"How much is my monthly payment?"
"How much do I need to save for college?"
"How do I save for a house?"

What do you notice about these questions? There's nothing wrong with them, per se. They're just not the right questions for generating true wealth. These questions focus primarily on spending and saving. They sound like the standard questions you'd find on a bank's website.

Financial institutions give us the information with which we make our money decisions. No wonder they're so popular. People have been blindly following this routine for years. Remember, banks are focused on plugging you into THEIR system, where THEY benefit the most. True wealth strategies, however, revolve around having your money work for YOU through your own system, where YOU are your own bank, and YOU benefit the most. You have to think differently and have a mindset shift if you want to get ahead of the herd.

"CASH SOLVES A LOT OF PROBLEMS. ACCESS TO CAPITAL IS CRITICAL."

—PHIL BODINE

WE NEED TO ASK THE RIGHT QUESTIONS

Wealthy-minded people ask themselves an entirely different set of questions. In the prologue of this book, I listed ten really good questions in the Financial Gear Test. (If you skipped taking it, I'd encourage you to go back and do so now.)

My hope is the quiz forces you to second-guess the long-held assumptions that most Americans have regarding money. Don't worry. As we continue to move forward, we'll dig deep and discover the truth about each one of those questions. Let me share a few additional questions I always ask when any investment or financial opportunity crosses my path, what I call the **5-Way Test**. I use these questions to make wise and prudent financial decisions, and I want to teach you to do the same.

THE 5-WAY TEST

(ASK THESE QUESTIONS IN THIS ORDER)

1. Is it LIQUID?

How easily can I convert my asset or security into readily available cash without affecting its market price? Owning equity is good, but not if I can't gain access to it without a penalty or a loss of value.

2. Does it offer SAFETY?

Will my principal investment be safe from losing value during down markets or uncontrollable circumstances? What are the downside risks?

3. What is the RATE OF RETURN?

Can I compute the net gain or loss of an investment over a specified time period? Or am I just guessing and hoping for the best?

4. Are there any TAX BENEFITS?

Will my actions increase or reduce the amount of taxes I pay? My desire is to reduce my taxes as much as possible or, ideally, pay no tax at all.

5. What is the EXIT STRATEGY?

Before you invest in anything (stocks, bonds, real estate, gold), you must ask yourself, "What's the exit strategy?" Most investments are all about the loading phase. Very few explain or even have an exit strategy. What good is an investment if the actual benefit works against you when you're ready to cash it out?

Liquidity, Safety, Rate of Return, Tax Benefits, and **Exit Strategy. These** are the five key points I hope to embed in your mind. Learning to filter your financial decisions through the right questions is foundational for moving forward on your road to true wealth.

Peak Performance Tip #3

Banks are businesses focused on plugging you into **THEIR** system, where **THEY** benefit the most.

WEALTH IN OVERDRIVE® STRATEGIES revolve around having **YOUR** money work for **YOU** through **YOUR** own system, where **YOU** are your own bank, and **YOU** benefit the most.

FOUR

LET ME ENTERTAIN YOU

THE SECRET OF SHOWMANSHIP CONSISTS NOT OF WHAT YOU REALLY DO, BUT WHAT THE MYSTERY-LOVING PUBLIC THINKS YOU DO.

—HARRY HOUDINI

Like many families in the Midwest, we were regular church attenders. The stories and sermons I heard helped shape who I am today. I'll never forget an old story I once heard about a frustrated preacher who, after finishing his sermon, stood at the pulpit and complained, "I am the minister of this congregation, and I make $400 a week. And that is not enough!"

This prompted the deacon of the church to stand up and proclaim, "Well, I am the deacon of this church, and I make $300 a week. And that is not enough!"

Then, the church secretary stood up and also chimed in. She said, "I'm the church secretary, and I make $200 a week. And that is not enough!"

Finally, the organist of the church stood up and announced, "I am the organist of this church, and I make $1,000 a week, and … **THERE'S NO BUSINESS LIKE SHOW BUSINESS!**"

Let's face it. We live in an entertainment-driven culture. Think about some of the words that have become part of our regular vocabulary in the past decade: Netflix, YouTube, Facebook, Paramount+, streaming, Xbox, Hulu, Spotify, Disney+, Twitch, HBO, social media, TikTok, and Amazon Prime, just to name a few. The entertainment industry is booming!

Between television, movies, music, video games, sporting events, theme parks, podcasts, summer festivals, and social media, it never ends. We are bombarded 24/7. Entertainment has permeated its way into nearly every aspect of our society … including the financial world.

There may be financial so-called "experts" who have written New York Times bestsellers or even have their own podcasts, radio, and TV shows, but saying you're an expert and being one are two different things. Being good at marketing and entertaining doesn't necessarily make people like these your best options for pursuing real wealth strategies.

Now, if you're trying to get your finances in order, construct a basic budget, or simply get out of debt, there are many financial celebrities who might be your ticket. But they tend to lead with a scarcity mindset, and I'm trying to help you build real wealth.

Philosophies like "all debt is bad" or "spend less money" will only get you to a certain level. It's like building with LEGOs. They can be a lot of fun, and you can even learn some things using them. But LEGOs are probably not the best option for building your dream house.

"BEWARE OF POPULAR ADVICE!

ADVICE DOESN'T HAVE TO BE CORRECT TO BE POPULAR."

—PHIL BODINE

I would rather you take advice from a registered, licensed, credentialed professional than media entertainers. After all, would you go to a doctor without an M.D. after their name? Would you go to a dentist who didn't graduate from dental school? Because a lot of these folks aren't registered licensed professionals, they have the ability to say whatever they want to say and to make blanket statements that many of us in the industry would never be allowed to say without getting warned or even fined. They don't have to worry about having their license revoked because they don't have one!

Financial entertainers seldom, if ever, talk about things like cash flow, leveraging inflation to your advantage, or developing multiple rates of return on your money. Instead, they try to convince people to believe the Wall Street formula, where **M**oney x **R**ate x **T**ime (**MRT** formula) is the answer. This formula is flawed because if you don't have enough money, aren't willing to take enough risk, and don't have enough time, it simply won't work. *Remember, when you are deceived, you think that wrong is right.* And financial entertainers are experts at pulling off this kind of sleight-of-hand magic.

Some financial entertainers also like to postulate about investments based on the **AVERAGE** rate of return. A long-term investment based on an average rate of return involves simple math. It's fun, appealing, and easy for a reader to grasp. **ACTUAL** rate of return, however, is a bit more complicated and not nearly as promising, as you'll see in Chapter 6. Markets tend to climb gradually and correct themselves abruptly, making the results of an average rate of return much more appealing than the results produced from the actual rate of return. And, unfortunately, in the real world, your investments will generate or lose money based on what's actually happening, not what is averaged out.

To propose an investment strategy that reaps a 12% average rate of return is not only pie-in-the-sky but delusional. There's a drastic difference between average rate of return and actual rate of return. This doesn't even take into account taxes, fees, or risk! We're talking about the difference between the hundreds of thousands of dollars proposed. I hope you had a good time reading their books because your retirement may not be as enjoyable. As the joke goes, "One day, I'm going to retire and live off my savings. However, I'm not sure **WHAT** I'm going to do the **NEXT** day."

It never ceases to amaze me how many misinformed people cross my path. It confirms my theory that advice doesn't have to be right to be popular. And just because it's popular certainly doesn't mean it's the best advice—all the dogs barking up the same tree doesn't mean it's the right tree. The fact of the matter is I've worked with many of the wisest and smartest financial advisors in the country who are highly specialized and have names that are virtually unrecognizable to the general public.

In short, just beware—the best marketers typically do not make the best financial advisors.

Peak Performance Tip #4

BEWARE OF FINANCIAL ENTERTAINERS

with a **SCARCITY MINDSET** who give generic, blanket, personal opinions to the masses rather than tailored professional advice to the individual.

"SO WHAT DO YOU BELIEVE BUILDS **MORE WEALTH**? **INCREASING** THE RATE OF RETURN, TAKING MORE RISK, OR **DECREASING** THE COSTS AND **ECONOMIC THREATS** TO BUILD THAT WEALTH?"

—PHIL BODINE

FIVE

THE INTERESTING TRUTH ABOUT COMPOUND INTEREST

AN INVESTMENT IN KNOWLEDGE PAYS THE BEST INTEREST.

—BENJAMIN FRANKLIN

Growing up with a strong desire to make money and get ahead, invariably, you hear a lot about compound interest. For me, as a young man, it was a mesmerizing concept. It seemed so logical and practical yet baffling. If compound interest was such a good idea, why wasn't everyone doing it? What was I missing? It reminds me of an old logic puzzle called the MISSING DOLLAR riddle. Perhaps you've heard of it before. It goes something like this …

Three guests checked into a hotel room. The manager charged them $30 for the room, so each guest paid $10. Later, the manager realized that the bill should have only been $25. To rectify his mistake, he gave the bellhop five $1 bills to return to the three guests.

On the way to the room, the bellhop realized that he couldn't equally divide the five $1 bills among the three guests. Since the guests were not aware of the revised bill, the bellhop decided to give the guests just $1 each and keep the remaining $2 as a tip for himself.

Since each guest got $1 back, they essentially paid $9 each for the room, bringing the total amount paid to $27 (3 x $9). The bellhop kept $2 for himself, which, when added to the $27, brings the total to $29.

So, if the guests originally handed over $30, what happened to the remaining dollar? Hence, the MISSING DOLLAR riddle.

While this riddle may seem baffling, it really comes down to how you look at it. Math is simple, logical, and linear. When we start throwing people, bellhops, and tips into the mix, it gets confusing. Renowned statistician John Tukey once said, "An approximate answer to the right question is worth a great deal more than a precise answer to the wrong question."[6]

In the case of the MISSING DOLLAR riddle, we are asking the wrong question. We're trying to figure out why (3 x $9) + $2 doesn't equal $30. In other words, we're looking at it the wrong way. The solution is as simple as this: the hotel manager has $25 in the register, the bellhop has $2 in his pocket, and the guests have $3 returned to their room: $25 + $2 + $3 = $30, the original amount paid.

If only investing were that simple. Unfortunately, many people look at investing the wrong way, and they ask the wrong questions. They want to believe it's simple math. If they invest $1,000 at 6% interest, in 12 years, they will have $2,000 because of that wonderful phenomenon known as compound interest! I heard it once said, "Compound interest is the eighth wonder of the world. He who understands it, earns it. He who doesn't, pays it."

It all seems so smooth and romantic. Banks, insurance companies, and multi-level marketing groups love to gush about the miracle of compound interest as if they've just discovered the cure for cancer. But financial institutions have an ulterior motive. If they can convince you that compound interest is the key to your financial success, you'll leave your money with them for as long as possible—maybe even forever. And in the end, you'll find yourself missing out on a lot more than simply a dollar.

ECONOMIC THREATS

For compound interest to work, you must keep the money in the investment for a long period of time without withdrawals or disruption. We need to look at the much bigger picture when it comes to the value of money by examining these eroding factors of money.

Circumstantial Threats

If I gave you five orange seeds today to plant in the ground with the hope of reaping a massive return in twenty years, you'd have to take your geographical location into account before you could ever expect to see a grove of orange trees coming up from the ground. If you lived in Florida, that'd be fine. Simple math suggests that five orange seeds planted in the ground x twenty years = orange trees. However, if you lived in Minnesota, you can throw this math equation out the window. Circumstantial factors like snow and sub-zero weather conditions would never allow the seeds to produce orange trees.

Life is full of circumstances that must be considered when investing in wealth building. Everyone has a unique set of situations, environments, and objectives that are distinctively different. Math has no such circumstantial factors. Math is a science. Two plus two will always equal four, no matter how or when you calculate it, because there are no eroding factors in math. It's just numbers. In real life, conditional variables are always part of the equation, especially when it comes to money.

Eroding Threats

Let's go back to our orange example. If I gave you five oranges and you set them on your patio table where they remained untouched, how many oranges would you have in thirty years? Simple math would conclude that you would still have five oranges. But in reality, you would have zero oranges. They would have decomposed and rotted away. Math doesn't take eroding factors into account. Money does.

Inflation decreases the value of money over time. For example, would you rather have $10,000 today or $10,000 thirty years from today? Obviously, you'd rather have it today because in thirty years you wouldn't be able to buy as much. To give you some perspective, thirty years ago, a McDonald's hamburger was just $0.72. Today, that same hamburger will cost you $2.79.[7] Your money will always buy more today than it will in the future because of inflation.

Remember, those who don't know what to do usually don't do anything. Whether you realize it or not, doing nothing is still a decision. And when you don't do anything, you drift along and get caught in the currents of inflation, taxes, and all the wealth-eroding factors. You'll never get to your destination. You'll be like a twig meandering aimlessly down a stream.

"FOR **COMPOUND INTEREST** TO WORK, YOU MUST KEEP THE **MONEY** IN THE INVESTMENT FOR A **LONG PERIOD** OF TIME **WITHOUT WITHDRAWALS OR DISRUPTION**."

—PHIL BODINE

External Threats

Real life is filled with things beyond our control, and they are seldom considered when crunching compound interest numbers. The COVID pandemic in 2020 impacted our economy in ways that were impossible to calculate in advance.

The same thing happened with the Twin Towers attacks on September 11, 2001. War, natural disasters, economic downturns, and other external factors all play a role in our lives and directly impact the outcome of our investments. Even something as simple as the commodity price of corn, sugar, and wheat will vary every hour, every day, because of external factors. Simply put, money fluctuates due to external factors (many of which are out of control). Math does not.

Tax Threats

Let me ask you a question: Do you think your taxes will be lower, the same, or higher in the future? Everyone usually laughs when I ask that question because they almost all expect taxes to rise in the future. This is especially true if your income grows over the course of your working life.

Taxes will play a significant role in determining the bottom line of your compound interest expectations. And even though there are strategies to combat taxes, most people are unaware of them. More likely, they've never seriously considered the tax aspect of compound interest in the first place. They simply fall in love with the pot of gold presented at the top of the compound interest mountain charts we have all seen.

Lost Opportunity Cost Threats

Aside from the need to secure a solid and consistent rate of return, the compound interest miracle requires one significant component to take place for success—your money must stay in the account. Compound interest doesn't work unless it stays in the plan, which means the money is not readily available to you.

It doesn't matter what opportunity comes down the pike—an amazing investment opportunity, a once-in-a-lifetime business partnership offer, or an incredible real estate deal, your compound interest money is off-limits. So, unless you're planning on breaking your compound interest streak, you'd better have another source of cash flow. Otherwise, you can kiss those opportunities goodbye.

Math doesn't include the real-life lost-opportunity-cost aspect of tying up funds with a long-term compound interest commitment.

Other Threatening Factors

Many other factors impact the value of money. Just take a look at some of the variables life throws at us, not to mention government policies, financial institutions, and large corporations.

If it sounds like I'm sour on compound interest, I'm not. It's a fascinating concept. My reservations lie in the fact that compound interest presents an incomplete promise that fools a lot of people into embracing a false hope without full disclosure of what actually lies ahead. And more importantly, there are smarter ways to invest.

Don't be hypnotized by the numbers. You rarely get what you are promised. It's not until you take a look at compound interest from a macro level, with all the deferred taxes and fees and lost opportunity costs involved, that you begin to truly understand it's all a hoax.

OTHER THREATS IMPACTING THE VALUE OF MONEY

PERSONAL LIFE	GOVERNMENT	FINANCIAL INSTITUTIONS	LARGE CORPORATIONS
Job Loss	Federal Income Tax	Sales Commissions	Price Increases (Inflation)
Disability	State Income Tax	Financial Fees	Reduced Product Quantity
Lawsuit	Local Income Tax	Loan Interest	Reduced Product Quality
Divorce	Capital Gains Tax	Insurance Premiums	Planned Obsolescence
Death	Real Estate Tax	Market Volatility	Technological Changes
Health	Sales Tax	Market Losses	Technological Service
Long-Term Care	Excise Tax	Credit Cards	Expiration Dates
Natural Disasters	Social Security Tax	Inappropriate Advice	False Advertising
Inflation	Estate Tax	Bad Financial Products	Pricing Policies
Cyber Scam/ Identity Theft	Devaluation of Money	Withdrawal Penalties	Wage Policies

The most interesting truth about compound interest is that it grooms people into asking the wrong questions:

"How many years do I have to keep my money in there?"
"What's the interest rate?"
"How much will it be worth at the end?"

But as we've already discussed in Chapter 3, the right questions to ask come from the **5-Way Test:**

"Is it **LIQUID?**"
"Does it offer **SAFETY?**"
"Can the **RATE OF RETURN** be calculated?"
"Are there any **TAX BENEFITS?**"
"What is the **EXIT STRATEGY?**"

If you continue asking these questions, you will go far. Attaining real wealth requires much more than following the allure of a simple "Money x Rate x Time" formula. It means educating yourself on how money can work to your advantage, recapture unwanted costs, and avoid economic threats, thus creating a more efficient way to optimize your full wealth potential.

Peak Performance Tip #5

Remember that in real life, **CONDITIONAL VARIABLES** and **ECONOMIC THREATS** are always important factors in the equation, especially when it comes to money.
IT'S NOT JUST ABOUT THE RATE OF RETURN.

Connect With Us!

If you would like to subscribe to the **Wealth in Overdrive**® podcast, keep up to date with future events and **Wealth in Overdrive**® workshops, or set up a one-on-one consultation with one of our registered team members, simply scan the QR code below.

SIX

WHAT TO DO IF YOU'RE PROMISED A 12% AVERAGE RATE OF RETURN ... RUN!

FOLLOWING THE CROWD IS NOT A WINNING APPROACH TO LIFE. IN THE END, IT'S A LOSER'S GAME.

—TIM TEBOW

One of the most important lessons I learned had to do with the phrase "average rate of return." It was almost magical, as clients seemed enamored with those four words. In 1993, a book titled *Magic Eye* was released, generating a pop-culture craze that revolved around optical illusions. The book displayed a gallery of two-dimensional pictures, each one containing a hidden three-dimensional image within. To discover the mystery figure, the viewer was required to position his eyeballs in such a way that he practically had to see through, or even enter, the picture itself. When he did, the illusion would materialize right in front of him. It was both challenging and captivating. The book's subtitle was *A New Way of Looking at the World.*

And now I'm about to show you a new way of looking at rate of return that is both challenging and captivating. Rate of return is a popular phrase for investors. We all want a good return on our investment. So, it certainly makes sense that we are concerned with the rate. The higher the rate, the better the return, right?

Unfortunately, the amount of attention paid to rate of return, in general, is out of balance. It's like a football coach who is only concerned about offense. He's not seeing the big picture. The same is true in the financial world. The rate of return doesn't tell the entire story. But most people don't know what they don't know.

Financial institutions and advisors capitalize on this. They have conditioned us to fall in love, not just with the rate of return, but with the AVERAGE rate of return, also known as ARR. We see this on almost every chart, prospectus, or promotion involving investments. It's all about the average rate of return. Even though it's deceiving, it's common practice in the industry.

Since the goal of an institution is to tie up your money for as long as possible, it only makes sense to promote the average rate of return because let's face it—some years are better than others. Markets tend to climb at a gradual pace. But when they correct themselves, the drop can be violent. Those market movements have a significant impact on the **actual** rate of return, making the average rate of return a much more appealing selling point to the prospective investor. If a company can promote a 10% average rate of return on your money over a 30-year period, the company suddenly appears stable, safe, and sound. Keep in mind that past performance is not an indication of future returns.

The average rate of return is espoused so confidently that it's become a stamp of stability. If there's a high average rate of return, it's got to be good. No need to question it. It's similar to the way we use brand names in place of the product they represent. For example, when I say "jacuzzi," you invariably think of a hot tub. But Jacuzzi isn't a company that only makes hot tubs. They also make mattresses, bathtubs, saunas, and massage chairs. The same goes for words like Jet Ski, Bubble Wrap, Kleenex, Sharpies, Q-Tips, and Weed Eaters. Those are all company brand names, not products. Don't believe me? Just Google it.

The average rate of return has that same level of familiarity in our minds. It's ingrained to the point where we don't even give it a second thought. We immediately associate it with being a benchmark for the success of our investments.

THE FINANCIAL MIRAGE

As I said earlier, **average** rate of return is not the same as **actual** rate of return. They are quite different. Let me show you what I mean.

If I promised you a 25% average rate of return on your investment, how much money would you give me? You'd probably give me as much as you possibly could. But let's play this out by doing the math with a simple example.

If you handed me $10,000 on January 1 to invest for you, and the first year yielded a 100% return, you'd be sitting at $20,000 by December 31. And that's not bad.

But year two wasn't quite as kind. Maybe it was a disaster. Your rate of return was -50%, shrinking your $20,000 back down to $10,000. That's a big bummer.

However, mathematically, the good news is that I kept good on my promise. 100% + (-50%) = 50%. Divide that by two years, and you get an average rate of return of 25%. The math cannot be disputed—that's the way we were taught how to calculate average rate of return.

AVERAGE ANNUAL RATE OF RETURN

YEAR	BEGINNING BALANCE	RETURN	ENDING BALANCE
1	$10,000	100%	$20,000
2	$20,000	-50%	$10,000

$$\text{AVERAGE ANNUAL RATE OF RETURN} = \frac{(100\%) + (-50\%)}{2 \text{ (YEARS)}} = \mathbf{25\%}$$

WHAT YOU'RE SHOWN ISN'T ALWAYS WHAT YOU GET!

But how can that be? You're sitting back at square one with your original $10,000 investment. Yet your average rate of return was 25%. That seems impossible!

I like to call it **the financial mirage. The reason is because math is not money, and money is not math.** Math is a science: 2+2 = 4, no matter how or when you calculate it. Money, on the other hand, is a commodity with all kinds of variables that need to be considered, such as the example of the oranges on the patio table in Chapter 5.

"MATH IS **NOT** MONEY, AND MONEY IS **NOT** MATH."

— ROBERT CASTIGLIONE

Average rate of return is found by simply totaling the rate of return from each year in a given period and then dividing that sum by the total number of years.

Actual rate of return, however, is the actual increase in value over that period divided by the number of years. So, in our example, the average rate of return is 25%. But the actual rate of return is 0% (actual increase is 0, divided by 2 years = 0). Now, do you see why average rate of return is promoted so enthusiastically? It's much more appealing. And amazingly, it's rarely ever questioned.

You may think, "That was just a silly little example involving two years with over-exaggerated rates. Certainly, real-life numbers don't work that way. Please tell me that in the real world, the average rate of return and the actual rate of return produce similar results. They have to, don't they?"

Typically, they do not produce similar results. In the example below, over the 24-year period from 2000 to 2023, the average rate of return on the S&P 500 Index (a major market indicator) was 8.71%. The actual rate of return was 7.03%.

Using the average rate of return, a $100,000 investment in the year 2000 would have grown to $742,109 by 2023 (not counting eroding factors like fees, taxes, lost opportunity cost, and inflation).

But that same $100,000 investment based on the actual rate of return would have brought your total to $510,842. That's a difference of $231,267, or 31.2% less![8]

Is it any wonder why advisors promote average rate of return? It implies security, stability, and a much greater windfall in the end. However, the truth is, you'll never end up with what average rate of return implies. You'll only earn what the actual rate of return produces. Again, we didn't take into account taxes, fees, and lost opportunity costs. *Fiction vs. Fact is the difference between average rate of return vs. actual rate of return.*

AVERAGE vs. ACTUAL RATE OF RETURN
S&P 500 OVER 24 YEARS

YEAR	INDEX RETURN
2000	-9.10
2001	-11.89
2002	-22.10
2003	28.68
2004	10.88
2005	4.91
2006	15.79
2007	5.49
2008	-37.00
2009	26.46
2010	15.06
2011	2.11
2012	16.00
2013	32.39
2014	13.69
2015	1.38
2016	11.96
2017	21.83
2018	-4.38
2019	31.49
2020	18.40
2021	28.71
2022	-18.11
2023	26.29

AVERAGE RATE OF RETURN = 8.71%
2023: "GROWN" to $742,109

ACTUAL RATE OF RETURN = 7.03%
2023: REALITY $510,842

DIFFERENCE OF $231,267
31.2% less!

Source: Slickcharts.com/sp500/returns. As of May 2024.

WHEN YOU'RE DECEIVED, YOU THINK WRONG IS RIGHT!

I once walked off a stage after presenting this reality to 400 professional financial advisers. I was astounded at how many really smart advisors could be so incredibly misinformed. The concept of average rate of return is so ingrained in our way of thinking that even the

"FICTION VS. FACT IS THE DIFFERENCE BETWEEN AVERAGE RATE OF RETURN VS. ACTUAL RATE OF RETURN."

—PHIL BODINE

experts don't give it a second thought. It goes back to the old adage that advice doesn't have to be right to be popular. And quite frankly, sometimes, a lie is easier to tell than the truth is to explain.

It doesn't help that financial advisors are creatures of this system. They get paid to promote strategies that keep feeding money to the big financial institutions while generating high management fees for themselves. It is fiction. Don't be deceived. Average rate of return is really just an optical illusion.

Unlike the *Magic Eye,* you don't have to force yourself to look cross-eyed to discover this hidden mystery. However, you do have to begin looking at the world in a new way, from a different perspective, to succeed.

It's time to shift our focus from looking at the average rate of return to the bottom line. After all, our concern should be, "In the end, how much will my wealth increase?"

Peak Performance Tip #6

Remember, **AVERAGE** rate of return is not the same as **ACTUAL** rate of return.

What you are shown isn't always what you'll get.

SEVEN

WHY TERM LIFE INSURANCE IS A GREAT DEAL ... FOR THE INSURANCE COMPANY!

PRICE IS WHAT YOU PAY; VALUE IS WHAT YOU GET.
—WARREN BUFFETT

Despite the fact that no one seems to enjoy talking about insurance, I realized early in my career that I needed to get a good grasp on this product. At first glance, I was impressed by the affordability of term coverage compared to "regular" insurance. I kept thinking, "What am I missing?"

It felt like the story of the illusionist who worked on a cruise ship. One evening, he was performing in front of a particularly rough crowd. To make matters worse, there was a man in the audience with a parrot on his shoulder giving away all the performer's secrets.

Every time the magician did a card trick, the bird blurted out, "It's up his sleeve!" And every time he made something disappear, the bird would screech, "It's in the other hand!" And every time he would transform an object, the bird would exclaim, "He swapped it out of his pocket!"

As the crowd roared with laughter at the bird, the embarrassed magician became so infuriated that he pulled out a stick of dynamite, lit it, and blew up the ship!

When the smoke cleared, the magician found himself floating aimlessly in the sea, clinging to a wooden door, along with the disheveled parrot. It was like a scene right out of the movie Titanic. Neither he nor the bird said a word for what seemed like hours. Finally, the parrot turned, looked the magician straight in the eye, and said, "Okay, I give up. Where's the ship?"

While companies that sell term life insurance may not be magicians, don't be surprised if you find yourself drifting aimlessly someday, thinking, "Okay, I give up. Where's my money?"

For clarity's sake, a term life insurance policy is a contract through which a life insurance company agrees to pay a specific person, trust, or charity (also known as the beneficiary) an allotted amount of money upon a person's death. It's designed to provide financial security and peace of mind for the family in the event of an untimely death. Term life insurance policies are attractive because they offer large payouts for little cost. On the surface, they sound great. But in actuality, it's the insurance companies who are the real winners. Let's examine the four hidden costs of term life insurance and reveal why it's not a great long-term strategy.

FOUR HIDDEN COSTS OF TERM LIFE INSURANCE

COST #1: The Actual Premium

Every contract you purchase, whether a whole life or a term contract, has an actual price tag (known as the premium). And while term policies are less expensive upfront, they are not considered an asset, and they build no cash equity. They are basically a roll of the dice. You are handing over money and betting that you will die, and the insurance companies are betting you won't.

Every dollar you give the insurance company is no longer yours. It goes into the insurance company's account. There is no cash value accumulating for you. There is nothing to borrow against. There is no surrender amount.

If you stop paying, cancel your contract, or reach the end of the designated time frame (typically 10, 20, or 30 years), your peace of mind disappears. It's like leasing vs. buying—once the lease is up, you own nothing. Your money is gone, and there's nothing left to show for your years of contributing except an empty bag.

COST #2: The Rate Increases with Age

While term life insurance policies attract customers because of the inexpensive price, don't be fooled. The older you get, the more expensive they become. That's because mortality odds increase each year as people age. In other words, the older you get, the more likely you will die. The probability of you dying after age sixty-five is much greater than before age sixty-five. Surprise, surprise.

When renewing a term life insurance contract that has reached the end of its timeframe, the premium (your cost) will be adjusted based on your current age and health status, which can only mean higher rates. *Much higher rates.*

In fact, term policies are created to eventually outprice the client. The older you get, the less sense it makes for you to keep forking out thousands of dollars in anticipation of a justifiable payoff. Eventually, policies are dropped, and insurance companies are off the hook. As they say, term insurance policies are intentionally designed to expire before you do.

Actuaries design them that way so that insurance companies can remain profitable in order to actually payout death claims. And even if you are somehow able to keep your contract until you die, it will lose tremendous value over time. For example, let's say you purchase a $1,000,000, 20-year term contract. And let's pretend that inflation averages 4% a year over the next twenty years. In this instance, your contract would lose 56% of its value over that time frame. Because there's no growing cash value inside your contract, you're essentially paying for a product designed to depreciate (not a great way to build wealth).

And then, when it's time to renew, you'd have to pay a higher rate to get the same value you initially desired (if you even qualify). It's a game where the price can only go up, and the value can only go down.

COST #3: The Lost Opportunity Cost

Even if you purchase a simple, inexpensive 20-year term contract that provides nothing more than peace of mind, you're still paying for it with real money that came out of your pocket, money that could have been invested elsewhere.

At the end of twenty years, if the contract doesn't pay out, you're left with nothing to show for your investment. For the serious investor, money matters. Wealthy-minded people always ask themselves, "Are my dollars working *for* me or *against* me?"

"THE
BITTERNESS OF
POOR QUALITY
REMAINS LONG
AFTER THE
SWEETNESS OF
LOW PRICE IS
FORGOTTEN."

—BEN FRANKLIN
(VIA BILL MCFADDEN)

COST #4: The Loss of the Death Benefit (No Payout)

Peace of mind is a big deal. Fear sells. Take away the emotion, and the numbers are astounding. Insurance industry studies have shown that the probability of filing a death benefit claim under a term life insurance contract is highly unlikely. One particular study placed the number as low as 2%. How ironic is that? In what other area of your life would you pay money for a product with a 98% chance of it never being delivered? I can't think of any.

When people purchase term life insurance, they are purchasing a product that's almost guaranteed **NOT** to deliver, despite having a trigger event (their death) that **IS** guaranteed to happen. It creates a literal cash cow for the insurance companies. It would be like going to a casino and looking down at a roulette wheel, where all the squares are black except for two that are red, and you bet on red. The probability of you landing on red is slim to none.

Can you imagine running a business where people paid you money, and 98% of them received nothing in return? We're talking about a business where you simply collect money for a living. It seems too good to be true. Yet, for insurance companies, that is how term policies work.

WARNING!!! BEWARE OF THE CONSEQUENCES OF "BUYING TERM INSURANCE AND INVESTING THE DIFFERENCE" AS A LONG-TERM STRATEGY.

You'll hear this phrase used by many financial entertainers, but there are consequences to doing this. Here's an analogy. It's like having four quarters to invest—you throw one quarter away and hopefully invest the other three. But many people fall prey to spending the difference rather than investing it in a disciplined manner.

Now, despite the four reasons I've just explained, there are some instances when term life insurance can make sense. If a family budget is tight and cash flow is limited, term insurance makes a good stopgap. For example, when a healthy young couple starts out, and one spouse stays home to care for the kids, it may be wise to insure the breadwinner for twenty years with a term contract. Their younger age and good health would mean lower rates. And if a tragedy were to happen to the working spouse, the survivor wouldn't be left in a hardship situation. The payout could be used to cover everyday expenses, as well as childcare and education costs. It's basically catastrophic coverage that allows them to maintain their current lifestyle instead of losing everything if disaster strikes. We prefer to call it a short-term Band-Aid strategy.

You should also be aware of a product known as a convertible term contract. It works a lot like a lease with the option to buy. With a conversion-type contract, term insurance acts as an on-ramp. It provides protection early in life and allows you to transition into a permanent contract when the time is right without having to pre-qualify. This can be a big deal, especially if you experience health issues. One can use the conversion privilege to convert an expense into an asset. Why rent when you can own?

For example, I have a client who purchased a 10-year term contract. Over the next few years, he became significantly overweight and developed diabetes. As his 10-year contract was drawing to a close, he wanted to extend his contract for another ten years. The problem was he would have had to have gone through the pre-qualification underwriting process again, which would have included proof of insurability. With his current health status, he most certainly would have been denied coverage. However, because his term contract was a convertible plan, he could transition into a permanent contract without the involvement of an underwriter. In essence, his term contract became a permission slip that kept him covered as he turned an expense into an asset.

So yes, there are situations in life when owning a term life insurance contract for a short period of time can prove to be a wise move. However, it's important to remember the four costs:

* The Actual Premium
* The Rate Increases with Age
* The Lost Opportunity Cost
* The Loss of the Death Benefit (No Payout)

I like to refer to term insurance as a good short-term strategy but not necessarily a great long-term solution. When using this type of insurance as a tool, you may need more than a magic wand to come out ahead.

Peak Performance Tip #7

Since less than 2% of term life insurance policies ever pay a death benefit,
ONLY USE TERM LIFE INSURANCE AS A SHORT-TERM SOLUTION, not a long-term strategy.

EIGHT

ARE 15-YEAR MORTGAGES A GOOD DEAL? (YES! FOR THE LOAN COMPANY!)

DEBT KEEPS YOU STUCK IN THE TRAP OF USING YOUR FUTURE TO PAY FOR YOUR PAST.

—MARY HUNT

"I want to pay off my mortgage as soon as possible so I can retire."

This is one of the most popular myths most people believe. And one of the most common questions I get asked is, "Should I do a 15-year or a 30-year mortgage on my home?" Great question! Seems like a no-brainer. After all, aren't we taught that debt is bad? Isn't it taboo in the financial world to owe money, especially for a long time? Perhaps, on the surface. But if there's one thing I've learned in my journey, it's to look below the surface.

Take maggots, for example. There's probably not a more disgusting, revolting creature on the planet. They're creepy, slimy, and squirmy and can usually be found writhing through rotting food or decomposing roadkill. They have no legs and no real digestive system, but they do have mouths with hooks to help grab decaying flesh. As they ravage through their ill-begotten booty, they secrete fluid containing digestive enzymes to help them dissolve their foul meal. No wonder most people avoid maggots at all costs.

But believe it or not, maggots aren't all bad. They have been used to help solve crimes and improve compost piles. And their secretions have been known to help heal wounds. That's right. Their enzymes can reduce inflammation, eliminate bacteria, coagulate blood, and stimulate healing responses, which amazingly can save lives, limbs, and money!

What a great example of why we shouldn't judge a book by its cover. If we continue to turn our heads the other way and not explore new possibilities, we will miss out on valuable opportunities.

Debt is often viewed in the financial world like maggots. It's considered bad and something we should avoid at all costs. And while I will agree that our country has a massive debt problem, as do many families, all debt isn't bad. Let's take a look.

CLASSIFYING DEBT

In all my decades as a planner, I've found that debt is one of the most important yet misunderstood topics in the financial world. People are often afraid to talk about their debts because it can be embarrassing. **But there's a big difference between HAVING debt and being IN debt.** And often, the type of debt we have is more important

"THERE'S A **BIG** DIFFERENCE BETWEEN **HAVING** **DEBT** AND **BEING IN DEBT**."

—PHIL BODINE

than the amount. For example, $500,000 **SECURED DEBT** on a home (which has value and utility) is quite different from $500,000 **UNSECURED DEBT** on a credit card. That being said, I'd like to classify debt into three categories: bad debt, good debt, and better debt.

1. Bad Debt (Unsecured Debt)

Bad debt is debt that is *unsecured*, such as credit card debt, store credit, or cash advances. There's no redeeming value in racking up bad debt. Other than the products you've purchased and the "reward" points you may have earned, there's no real return on your investment. You may have had an enjoyable vacation, splurged on some good meals, or bought a new wardrobe, but once the dust settles, all you end up with is bad debt with really high-interest charges.

2. Good Debt (Secured Debt)

Then there's good debt. Good debt is *secured* by an asset, such as your house, which can and most likely will appreciate in value over time. Or it could be a student loan used to attain a degree that leads to improved knowledge, better marketability, and a larger income. These are all items that provide a clear and continuing benefit to you.

3. Better Debt (Secured Debt Cash Flow)

Finally, there's better debt. Better debt is *leveraged* in such a way that it adds capital and cash flow to your business or personal portfolio. It's designed to be a conduit for creating your own income stream. When it comes to the topic of better debt, I often think of the quote from Robert Kiyosaki, author of the best-selling book *Rich Dad Poor Dad*. He states, "How do I get rich? I borrow money, and I buy assets that create cash flow."

Many people have one, two, or all three types of debt in their lives. As a financial advisor working in a culture surrounded by debt, my job isn't simply to help clients get rid of their debt; it's to help them manage or transition their debt from bad to good or better.

For example, I have a client named Dr. Phil, who is a dentist in his early fifties. He had hoped to purchase a $60,000 digital equipment for his practice but wasn't sure if he should pay cash or finance it. Instead of paying cash, I had him give me the $60,000 to invest, and he chose to finance the equipment over ten years. As a result, he brought in $388,000 in business revenue and more than doubled his investment in his portfolio over that decade. This is a good example of better debt.

We know it makes sense to avoid bad debt. And better debt is certainly an option to consider when expanding your business or portfolio. But I've found that it's the good debt category that remains the most unrealized and untapped opportunity for financial gain. Quite simply, most people are unaware of the possibilities. While many Americans have purchased their home or vehicle on credit, these loans are typically viewed with disdain, like a necessary evil. In fact, it wasn't that long ago when people would often celebrate making their final house payment by throwing what was known as a "mortgage burning party." What many would consider a major accomplishment, I view as a missed financial opportunity. And it all begins with how we look at things.

A NEW PERSPECTIVE

If I were to say, "I've got an amazing investment opportunity," you might respond, "Terrific, what is it?"

And I'd say, "Well, let me just outline the parameters, and you can tell me how much you want to invest."

"Great! What are they?"

"Well, . . .

* You determine the amount and length of time for the contribution to continue.

* You can pay more than the minimum contribution, but not less.

* If you try to pay less, the financial institution keeps ALL of your previous contributions.

* The dollars you invest are not liquid.

* The dollars you invest will earn a zero percent rate of return.

* The money you deposit is NOT safe from loss of principal.

* Your tax liability will increase with each contribution you make.

* When your plan is finally completed, you will be paid no income.

"So, how much would you like to invest?"

You'd probably respond, "Nothing. Sounds like a horrible investment!"

And you would be correct. But, believe it or not, it's a way of life for millions of people. Guess what this investment is?

It's the mortgage on your home. It's hard to view a mortgage in such stark terms because we are conditioned to think of our mortgage as just a normal part of living. But from a financial perspective, the points I made are true.

→ **You get to determine how many years you want to regularly contribute.** You do this by choosing a 15-year, 20-year, or 30-year mortgage.

→ **You can pay more than the minimum contribution, but not less.** Banks encourage and love it when you pay extra! Paying less is not an option. In fact, it puts the bank in a safer position in the transaction, not you.

→ **If you do try to pay less than the originally agreed-upon contribution amount, the financial institution gets to keep ALL of your previous contributions.** Do you know what happens when you try to make a house payment for less than what's required? You go into foreclosure. The financial institution keeps all your previous contributions. That alone should tell you that home equity probably isn't the best place to storehouse your money.

→ **The dollars you invest are not liquid. The dollars in the account aren't liquid because you don't control them.** Who owns the money in your house? The bank does. There's no way to get to them. To access the money, you have to either sell the house or go back to the bank and pay them interest to borrow your money (home equity line of credit). Long story short, it's no longer your money.

→ **The dollars you invest will earn zero percent.** The dollars in the account earn a zero percent rate of return because you don't actually have dollars in the account. If you're talking about dollars in the house (also known as your equity), you are conceivably earning a return if the house increases in value. But don't kid yourself—there are no dollars in the account. Simply put, home equity will NEVER get a rate of return, no matter how much equity you have in your home. Home equity is based on the appraisal value of your home at the time of sale.

Home equity = appraisal value of your home - the debt

→ **It doesn't matter whether you have your house completely paid for or not.** If your house was paid off and you borrowed $50,000 of equity against the house to buy a car (not that you should), it won't affect the value of your house. And the reason it doesn't affect the value is because your house is a leveraged asset. **Therefore, in and of itself, home equity has no rate of return.** You save the interest you would have paid on the mortgage, but you end up forgoing the potential earnings on another investment.

→ **The money you deposit is NOT safe from loss of principal.** Could you lose the equity in your house? Absolutely. Remember the housing crash of 2008?

→ **Your tax liability will increase with each contribution you make.** Yes, your tax liability increases with each contribution. As you pay down the principal, the amount of interest included in each monthly payment decreases, meaning that the deduction you take for interest on your mortgage decreases, too.

→ **When your plan is finally completed, you will be paid no income.** When all is said and done, you're not getting any income for your efforts. The caveat here is yes, you could get some income—but not until you sell the house.

So, how much liquidity, use, and control of your money are you willing to lose?

Do you know the meaning of the word *mortgage?* "Mort" is a Latin word that means "death." And the Old French meaning of "gage" is "pledge." So, the word mortgage means "death pledge." Sounds pretty accurate to me. Once you take out a mortgage, it seems like you end up paying the bank until you die.

For the fun of it, let's apply the **5-Way Test** to a mortgage:

1. Is it **LIQUID?**
   No. The only way to get to your money is to sell the house or borrow against it.

2. Does it offer **SAFETY?**
   No. And extra payments won't help.

3. Can the **RATE OF RETURN** be calculated?
   No. As I just explained, there is no rate of return on a home mortgage. Your house is a leveraged asset.

4. Are there any **TAX BENEFITS?**
   Yes. However, the more payments you make, your tax liability increases.

5. Is there a successful **EXIT STRATEGY?**
   No. Typically, there is no exit strategy involved with a mortgage other than to hand your money over to the bank, no questions asked.

   Your mortgage just failed four out of the five questions.

WHAT ABOUT THE 15-YEAR MORTGAGE?

So, how do we use good debt in a way that works in our favor as a financial planning strategy? It would seem that converting a 30-year mortgage into a 15-year mortgage might save thousands of dollars. We've all seen the flyers. Banks promote the 15-year mortgage by getting people to focus on how much they'd save in interest if they were to pay off their house in half the time. But let me ask you a question … if 15-year mortgages will save people thousands of dollars, why are lending companies so eager to promote them? They can even entice you with a lower interest rate. Doesn't that seem strange to you?

You might argue, "Wait … I thought you said that banks want to hang onto my money as long as possible. Wouldn't it make more sense for them to promote a 30-year mortgage?"

The truth is, banks actually want you to convert your 30-year mortgage to a 15-year mortgage for a couple of reasons. First off, the shorter term obligates you to make higher payments, increasing the chance of foreclosure and thus giving the bank a shot at keeping your down payment. Banks actually *want to lend you* the money and get it back as quickly as possible.

But even more importantly, higher payments mean more money coming into the bank, which it can then loan out to other customers and make even more money. In other words, you're giving the bank the opportunity to capitalize on your money. Remember, the bank owns the money in the home, not you.

In 2017, Warren Buffett called the 30-year mortgage the "best instrument in the world." He may be right because if for no other reason, a 30-year mortgage allows you to **leverage inflation to your benefit**. A $3,000 house payment today won't be nearly as hard to make thirty years from now. Why not? Because $3,000 won't be worth nearly as much.

So if your money is worth more today, why would you want to take those more valuable dollars and sink them into a home? We've already talked about why a home isn't a great investment vehicle. It makes much greater financial sense to invest your extra payment money into something liquid that offers safety, has a rate of return, produces tax benefits, and provides a sound exit strategy. I actually have clients who, in the course of paying off their 30-year mortgage, leveraged inflation to their benefit. By year thirty, their biggest complaint was that their utility bill was larger than their house payment. It's too bad we can't leverage inflation to offset all our costs in life. But as long as 30-year mortgages are available, why in the world wouldn't we use them to our advantage when it comes to purchasing our homes?

Did you know that in France and Spain, they offer a 50-year mortgage option? And believe it or not, Switzerland and Japan offer 100-year options! That may seem insane. But if offered in the United States, I'd take one out and pay the minimum required each month. I know this sounds counterintuitive to most Americans, but you have to remember that every dollar you own should be treated as one of your employees. Do you want your employees working for the bank or for you? It's about cash flow, not about the type of mortgage.

Financial entertainers love to promote the idea of having absolutely no debt by making statements such as, "All debt is bad" and "Get out of debt as soon as you can!" But think about that for a second. Let's pretend that you have a home worth $500,000. And you also own a portfolio of CDs worth $500,000. On the asset side of your net worth statement, you'd have $1,000,000. And on the liability side of your statement, you'd have $500,000 (your mortgage). If net worth equals assets minus liabilities, your net worth would be $1,000,000 – $500,000 or $500,000.

NET WORTH STATEMENT

ASSETS	LIABILITIES
$500,000 (HOME)	$500,000 (MORTGAGE)
$500,000 (PORTFOLIO)	

NET WORTH (ASSETS - LIABILITIES) = $500,000

So, if we follow the advice that all debt is bad and we should get out of debt as soon as possible, why not take the $500,000 in CDs and simply pay off the mortgage? Now we're completely out of debt. Seems like the smart thing to do. It even feels pretty good. What's the problem?

NET WORTH STATEMENT

ASSETS	LIABILITIES
$500,000 (HOME)	~~$500,000 (MORTGAGE)~~
~~$500,000 (PORTFOLIO)~~	

NET WORTH (ASSETS - LIABILITIES) = $500,000

Do the math. We now have $500,000 on the asset side of our net worth statement and zero on the liability side ($500,000 – 0 = $500,000). It's the exact same net worth as before! You paid down your mortgage to experience the American dream, but in actuality, you've created the American nightmare. **You're house rich and cash poor!** You've done nothing to change your net worth. **YOUR HOUSE IS BALANCE SHEET NEUTRAL.** Paying off debt is not the same as accumulating assets.

On the net worth statement, it doesn't matter if the liability is wiped out or not. You're still worth the same amount on paper. But what you have done is eliminated all your investment flexibility by turning your investable assets over to the bank. You cut the asset side in half. They now control your money, and they are in a much better financial position than you are.

A much wiser strategy would be to pay off your house on the **OUTSIDE** rather than on the **INSIDE**. That means it's smarter to invest your money in assets that will accumulate to the point where you could pay off your home if you wanted to in a more efficient way, but instead, you retain control. It's more prudent to keep your dollars working for you on the outside instead of being held prisoner on the inside, where the banks will put them to work for their own gain.

HOMES ARE MEANT TO HOUSE FAMILIES, NOT STORE CASH.

The most overlooked reasons to keep a 30-year mortgage instead of a 15-year mortgage are liquidity, cash flow, and tax advantages. For many families, the interest portion of their mortgage payment sometimes represents their largest tax write-off. By paying off a home early, that luxury is essentially eliminated!

DON'T GET THE OBJECTIVE CONFUSED WITH THE METHOD.

I realize that looking at debt and mortgage payments in this new light is a huge paradigm shift for most people. But when creating real wealth, you have to see things differently. In other words, you have to see maggots as life savers.

Peak Performance Tip #8

Remember, there's a **difference between HAVING DEBT** and being **IN DEBT**.

Not all debt is bad debt.

NINE

WHAT'S THE DEAL WITH INSURANCE DEDUCTIBLES?

WHEN DEALING WITH PEOPLE, REMEMBER YOU ARE NOT DEALING WITH CREATURES OF LOGIC, BUT CREATURES OF EMOTION.

—DALE CARNEGIE

I'll never forget the day I bought my first car. I was twenty years old, and I paid cash for a used four-door '81 Honda Civic. It was a five-speed with really high mileage, and I was prouder than a peacock. But then I realized I had another decision to make: "Should I choose a low deductible or a high deductible on my car insurance?"

That's a common question nearly everyone who drives has to figure out. And the selection you make reveals your philosophy or understanding of money. For clarity's sake, a deductible is the amount of money you pay out of your own pocket before the insurance company starts paying for damage due to an accident. As a simple example, if you had a car accident that put your car in the shop with $2,000 worth of damage, and the deductible on your car insurance was $500, you'd be responsible for the first $500 portion of the bill, while the insurance company would owe the remaining $1,500.

The selection of a high versus low deductible is made at the time you purchase your car insurance contract. And this is where most people struggle. Is it smart to pay more upfront with a low deductible? Or is it wiser to save money on the front end by purchasing a contract with a high deductible?

On one hand, dealing with the immediate concerns of a car accident is already hard enough emotionally. Why compound the problem with financial stress? It would be nice to know that your car is taken care of in case the worst happens. Better go with the low deductible.

On the other hand, it sure seems to cost a lot more to have that extra peace of mind. Is it really worth it? Can you actually put a dollar amount on peace of mind?

The better question you might want to ask is, "What kind of a deductible do financial institutions want me to have?" Remember their motivation? They want to control as much of your money as possible. That means their desire is for you to pay a higher premium by going with the low deductible. That should be your first red flag.

But let's just take a pragmatic look at the numbers and see if a low deductible actually is a better value than a high deductible. A sampling of auto insurance companies shows that having a low deductible, such as $250, will cost you roughly $180 more annually than if you have a high deductible of $1,000. So essentially, you are spending $180 more for an extra $750 worth of coverage ($1,000 - $250).

If you seem to have a lot of car accidents, get the low deductible. But most people go years, if not decades, without having a major accident. The car insurance industry estimates that the average driver will file a claim for a collision about once every 17.9 years. Do the math. If you spend an additional $180 each year during that 17.9-year period, you will shell out an extra $3,222 for that ancillary $750 worth of protection. That's not a great deal for you. It is, however, great for the insurance company.

Take a look at the big picture. Your ultimate goal should be to protect yourself against a large financial liability that could cripple you for life. With a high deductible, you've accomplished that goal. You are protected from a major personal financial collapse. Should an accident happen, having to pay a $1,000 deductible out of your pocket might be inconvenient, but it won't ruin your financial future. You want to protect yourself from catastrophes, not inconveniences. Why not take the $180 you save every year and put it to work for you so that when an accident does occur, you've got more than enough to make up for the $750 benefit you missed out on?

Or better yet, consider purchasing an **umbrella liability policy**. For $200 to $350/year, you can buy a million dollars of liability protection and take advantage of the biggest bargain in the insurance world. An umbrella policy kicks in after you have used up the underlying coverage on the primary contract of your automobile (or home). This type of contract is capable of much broader coverage, often including things like bodily injury, property damage, personal injury, false arrest, false imprisonment, malicious prosecution, defamation, invasion of privacy, wrongful entry, and garnishment of wages for the rest of your life.

I play golf with attorneys, and they have always mentioned to me that this is the cheapest form of liability coverage given all circumstances to protect and insulate assets and future income from lawsuits. Spending the extra money on a liability umbrella policy is certainly more efficient than purchasing a lower deductible on your car insurance, one will save you a few hundred dollars. The other could save you up to one million!

Incidentally, the same philosophy holds true for homeowners insurance. Choosing the highest deductible available and putting the money you save to work for you is just smart money management. Agents love to sell the idea of peace of mind for the moment. But as a wise financial decision-maker, you're no longer looking at the moment. You're now looking at the big-picture master plan that is the most beneficial for you and your family.

Ultimately, true wealth is about retaining control of as much of your money as possible. Choosing the right deductible is part of that process.

Peak Performance Tip #9

Don't overpay for peace of mind.
Select the insurance option that offers the
**MAXIMUM AMOUNT OF PROTECTION
FOR THE LEAST AMOUNT OF COST.**

THE MOST TOXIC ASSET

IT'S BETTER TO WALK ALONE THAN WITH A CROWD GOING IN THE WRONG DIRECTION.
—DIANE GRANT

Another big lesson I learned had to do with products that are considered status quo, specifically 401(k) plans and IRAs. Even if you know next to nothing about financial planning, you've surely heard of these.

People often ask me why I am not a big fan of these plans. Let me ask you … have you ever taken an objective look at them? Here are a few noteworthy observations:

* You provide all the money to capitalize the plan.

* During this capitalization phase, the money isn't liquid.

* Your tax liability compounds with each contribution.

* You incur all the risk at all times.

* If you withdraw early, you will incur penalties.

* You agree to share a percentage of all profits or withdrawals.

* All agreed-upon rules and regulations are subject to change without your consent.

I'm not making this up. This is how almost all typical qualified 401(k) and IRA plans work. Why would anyone want to put their money into them under these conditions? Yet, they are some of the most popular "investments" on the planet.

We've been raised in a culture that says, "This is what everyone does. And if everyone does it, it has to be good." Ladies and gentlemen—we've been duped!

In my office, we often refer to these pre-tax contribution retirement schemes as **GOVERNMENT-SPONSORED PLANS**. How does that description sit with you? We call them government-sponsored plans because all the money you sink into them is no longer yours. It belongs to the government. The money is theirs (as in The**IRS**). In a 401(k), the government places a lien on their share of the plan from day one, as Uncle Sam puts an arm around your shoulder and becomes your financial partner. **Remember, you owed the tax the day you made the deposit.** You don't really own your plan; you're renting it from the government. The IRS is the general partner, and you're the limited partner, which really means you have no say so in the matter, and they can change the rules to their benefit at will. Even though these plans are promoted as the be-all, end-all for our financial future, they are a hoax.

"GOVERNMENT-SPONSORED PLANS = **YOU** OWE THE TAX THE DAY YOU **MAKE THE DEPOSIT**."

—PHIL BODINE

Let's consider again the **5-Way Test** for government-sponsored plans:

1. Is it **LIQUID**?
2. Does it offer **SAFETY**?
3. Can the **RATE OF RETURN** be calculated?
4. Are there any **TAX BENEFITS**?
5. Is there an **EXIT STRATEGY**?

Let's see. No, no, no, no, and no. A 401(k) fails every single one of these questions. These plans are both a win-win and a lose-lose. The winners are the IRS and the financial institution that manages your 401(k). The losers are you, the investor who funds the plan and takes all the risk, along with your beneficiaries.

When these plans originally came on the market, they were known as **Salary Reduction Plans.** That ought to tell you something. They were called Salary Reduction Plans because the amount that you contributed to your plan was deducted from your taxable income for the year. However, the name Salary Reduction Plan proved to conjure up negative images, so the plans were eventually rebranded by the IRS as 401(k)s. I like to call it **"The 401(k) Hoax."** A hoax is a humorous or malicious deception. It's an act intended to trick or dupe people. It's something that is accepted or established by fraud or fabrication. If you think I'm being too hard on 401(k)s, keep reading.

Qualified plans are promoted in such a way as to trick you into thinking that you won't have to pay taxes on all of your income. For example, if you earn $100,000 and put $10,000 into an IRA, you'll only have to pay taxes on $90,000. But that's not true. You've simply reduced your taxable salary for the current year. There were no tax savings! Just a reduction in income. Thus, the title Salary Reduction Plan. Uncle Sam hasn't forgotten about the other $10,000. He'll get his share and more at a later date. Yet somehow, we, as consumers, have all been led to believe that this is a good thing. For some reason, we think of the word "deferred" as a major bonus, almost as if it's synonymous with tax-free. But tax-deferred is really just another way of saying that your tax calculation and tax bill are postponed until a later date. And, unfortunately, it can be quite costly.

Your money is taxed when you withdraw your funds. The plans are also taxed when your remaining assets are passed on to your beneficiaries. And if the taxes haven't been paid by that time, your estate will pay the taxes. Somehow, some way, the taxes will be paid. There is nothing tax-free about typical 401(k)s or IRA plans. **IT'S REVERSE TAX PLANNING**. I like to use this quote by Ed Slott:

"An IRA is an IOU to the IRS."

—Ed Slott, CPA

Let me ask you this. Do you believe future tax rates will be …

LOWER? THE SAME? HIGHER?

Of course, no one really knows what the tax rates will be in the future. While paying taxes later sounds like a great idea, common sense indicates that taxes will be higher, not lower, as time marches on.

In our country, we have an aging demographic and unsustainable debt. Why would anyone want to shovel money into a plan that delays tax liability to a time in the future when it will likely be much higher? It doesn't sound like a winning strategy. And that's because it's not.

There's another factor at play that few people ever consider. It's been my experience that people somewhat understand the tax deduction but not the consequences of tax deferral. Take a look at this chart.

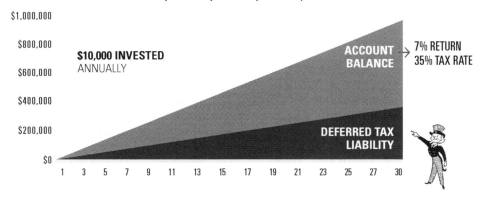

GOVERNMENT-SPONSORED PLANS
401(k), IRA, SEP, 457, 403(b)

$10,000 INVESTED ANNUALLY

ACCOUNT BALANCE → 7% RETURN 35% TAX RATE

DEFERRED TAX LIABILITY

As the graphic shows, if you invest $10,000/year and get a 7.5% annual return, you end up with $1.2 million after thirty years. That's not too shabby. But your earnings aren't the only thing compounding in the plan. **THE DEFERRED TAX LIABILITY CURVE IS COMPOUNDING IN TANDEM WITH YOUR EARNINGS!**

Essentially, the government has loaned you the tax to compound on their behalf at your expense. Is that a good thing or a bad thing? Every dollar you invest in one of these qualified plans increases your risk. You put yourself in a situation where your wealth can be snatched away with the simple stroke of a pen or any geopolitical event that results in higher taxes. You have no protection. *Remember, a deferred tax is nothing more than a compounded/larger tax at an uncertain rate in the future.* Would you rather pay a **KNOWN** tax today or have an **UNKNOWN** tax liability in the future? While it feels good to pay less today, all you're really doing is kicking the can a little farther down the road. If you were a farmer, would you rather pay a known tax rate now on $75/acre or pay an unknown tax rate later on $600/acre? In other words, is it smarter to pay tax on the **SEED** or the **HARVEST**?

WHICH TAX WOULD YOU RATHER PAY?

SOY BEANS EXAMPLE

It's almost always smarter to pay the taxes as you go along (on the seed) than it is to wait and pay your taxes at the end (on the harvest). By learning to annually invest your post-tax proceeds into a more productive vehicle, you'll have more money and fewer headaches in the long run. Plus, you'll be able to access your funds along the way—tax-free! This is a huge advantage when it comes to living in real time because life happens. This is a luxury that qualified plans do not offer because the funds are locked up in money jail. Have you ever tried using your 401(k) to cover an emergency expense? The penalties can be brutal. Which form of income would you rather have during your golden years of retirement? **FOREVER TAXED** or **NEVER TAXED**?

Plus, government-sponsored plans often lead to disaster when passed on to heirs. For example, if a couple wants to transfer a $500,000 IRA to their children, the financial advisor will typically try to dodge this bullet by saying, "Well, that's an estate planning question." The last thing the advisor wants to do is take the blame for the mess about to ensue. When the IRA is passed on to the children as part of the estate, it could be taxed at 40% to 55%. The kids, of course, still have to pay income taxes on what's left when they withdraw the money.

The fallacy of 401(k) plans is that we think we can build up our savings until we turn seventy-two and then withdraw money at will, spending as we wish. With Social Security and a possible pension in place, everything should be smooth sailing, right?

However, the most common question seventy-two-year-olds tend to ask is, "How do I stop those required minimum distributions from coming out of my IRA so I can keep my taxes from getting out of control?"

Government-sponsored plans could easily be called "Forever Tax" plans. They're kind of like the army: they're a lot easier to get into than to get out of. Once you sign up, you enter into a partnership with the IRS. It's the government's plan, not yours. They now get to call the shots. It's crazy.

IMAGINE GOING INTO A BANK, APPLYING FOR A HOME LOAN,

AND THEN ACTUALLY SIGNING FOR IT BLINDLY WITHOUT

KNOWING TWO CRITICAL FACTS:

1) THE RATE,

2) THE TERMS OF THAT AGREEMENT.

No one would do that. That would be ludicrous! Yet, for some reason, most people find it completely normal to shovel loads of cash mindlessly into their 401(k) with no idea what the rate and terms will be, how much they'll owe in taxes, or what kind of return they'll end up with at retirement. The government can change the rules anytime they wish. If they want to deduct a percentage from all plans to offset some of the national debt, they can do that. They can do whatever they want because it's their plan, not yours. The only time it becomes your money is when you pay the taxes and penalties to access your cash. Why would anyone enter into such an agreement?

My dad once told me, "Son, in life, you're going to make good decisions, and you're going to make bad decisions. Avoid the bad ones, especially the ones that will haunt you for the rest of your life."

Putting money into a government-sponsored plan is one of those decisions. It will haunt you. Yet it's a decision that almost all people make! It's a herd mentality that very few people ever question. And it's exactly what financial institutions desire.

Do you remember the four basic rules of financial institutions?

* They want all your money.
* They want it on a systematic, ongoing basis.
* They want to hold onto your money for as long as possible.
* And they want to give you nothing in return.

The 401(k) plan is the poster child for the philosophy above.

People love to debate me about these plans, especially when an employer match is involved. How can it be a bad deal if an employer will match your contribution? That has to change everything, right? The truth is that the employer often doesn't contribute the entire amount all at once. The company can spread the contribution match from four to six years and have it vest over time. If you leave your job before those six years are up, as is common, you often don't get the match; at best, you receive just the vested amount. When the dust settles, the employer is actually saving money in the long run by installing a 401(k) program. And even if you receive the match, remember, the money in the plan isn't yours. It belongs to the government. Essentially, the employer match will be used to pay the tax on your money and contributions when you withdraw it as income.

My wise mother was a victim of qualified plans. Her former financial advisor encouraged her to put a large portion of her money into a qualified plan he set up for her. Multiple years later, she needed $9,000 for medical expenses, so she withdrew it from her plan. At the end of the year, she had to pay more than she expected in taxes. Guess where she went to get the money to pay her tax bill? She withdrew more from her qualified plan. She got trapped into a vicious cycle that led her far from the financial promised land her advisor had promoted. It was a triple insult to injury!

This type of thing plays out every day in our country. I met with a client who had over $5.8 million in his qualified plan. He was an orthopedic surgeon getting ready to retire. As we reviewed his income sources, his accountant said, "Oh, he can't take that money out. He'll be taxed on it."

"What?!" I exclaimed. "Who advised him to deposit all this money into this plan?"

When I found out it was the accountant himself, I was outraged. What in the world is the purpose of a plan if you can't eventually use it? I'm certain the CPA thought of himself as a hero when the doctor made the contributions many years earlier.

Everyone seems to understand the concept of putting money aside for retirement, but far too few people think about the financial repercussions that will happen when it's time to withdraw. These plans are good accumulation vehicles, but they're deplorable tools for distributing funds, either to the investor or their heirs. Real planning involves thinking through the details. It takes work. It takes … well, very strategic thought and planning. Unfortunately, many of today's advisors quickly suggest, "Oh, just blindly throw your money in here, and I'll watch it grow and accumulate for you."

"THE GOVERNMENT **LOANS** YOU THE TAX DEDUCTION TO **COMPOUND** ON THEIR BEHALF **AT YOUR EXPENSE**."

–PHIL BODINE

It's not even the financial institution's money at risk. It's YOUR money at risk. This sounds harsh, but it's far more common than you'd want to imagine.

And here's a little secret about wealthy people. They have very little, if any, of their net worth locked up in qualified plans. They simply know better. Or they employ financial advisors who know better.

Other people learn the hard way. Years ago, I acquired clients from Chicago. They were retired professionals with three grown children, each with college degrees and families of their own. They looked forward to spending time and money on their grandkids.

At the time, they needed a new slate roof on their home. Water was leaking through their current roof and getting into the drywall. Mold began to appear and needed immediate attention or their home would be uninhabitable.

Do you know what the price tag was for their new slate roof? It was $90,000. Their previous advisor had not set up a contingency fund to help pay for life's unforeseen circumstances (i.e., the roof). The problem was they had to take out an extra $40,000 to pay for the tax they incurred for withdrawing the $90,000 to pay for the roof. That roof ended up costing them a total of $130,000 in distributions from their IRA! While other money was invested in stocks, they didn't want to cash out their portfolio. These were well-educated clients, but unfortunately, they had sunk most of their investable money and assets into their government-sponsored plan. They didn't want to withdraw their money, but it was their only real option. And they paid dearly for it.

Experience can be a brutal teacher. That seems to be the case with the man who originally developed the 401(k) as well. Years ago, a benefits consultant named Ted Benna realized that a clause in the Revenue Act of 1978 (section 401(k)) could be used for expanded purposes besides its original objective. He used this loophole to create a retirement savings vehicle for employees. Essentially, Benna discovered a tax-free way to defer employee bonuses and stock options.

Shortly thereafter, the IRS allowed 401(k)s to be used to defer regular wages as well. That's when the floodgates opened.

It wasn't until 2022 that Benna realized he had created a "monster." He said, "If I were beginning from scratch today, with what we know now, I'd blow up the existing structure and focus on how money is allocated."[9] In 2018, he commented, "I've documented the history of these plans and how participants have been impacted, and it's not a pretty picture. It went from all fees being paid by the employer to everything getting bundled and dumped on the employees."[10]

If the man who created these plans doesn't think they're any good, why should we? And if financial "experts" are so smart, why do they continue to promote them? Those are good questions to ponder.

"THE 401(k) IS A ROTTEN REPOSITORY FOR RETIREMENT RESERVES."

Time Magazine
"Why It's Time to Retire the 401(k)"
October 2009

So, what should you do if you have money tied up in such a plan? Given your past experience and what you have learned, ask yourself, "What is the wisest thing to do?" Is it smarter to take the funds out gradually or all at once? I've found that the one way to implement a "401(k) rescue strategy" is to rip the Band-Aid off. Take it all out, absorb the tax loss, and let the plan die. Also, there are other little-known provisions in the IRS tax code that give you the legal ability to harvest penalty-free withdrawals from your 401(k), even if you are younger than fifty-nine-and-a-half years old. It's called Internal Revenue Code section 72(t). Then, you can begin repositioning your money into more tax-efficient assets. It may be one of the smartest moves you make toward accumulating true wealth.

Author and CPA Bryan Bloom says, "Where your money resides is far more important than what it earns."[11] The key is to keep your money in motion. Don't let your employer hold your retirement assets hostage. **Remember, you don't need a retirement plan to retire. You need cash flow!**

For more on this topic, read our complimentary article called "401(k) A Good Investment?" by visiting the **Wealth in Overdrive**® website. Simply scan this QR code:

Peak Performance Tip #10

GOVERNMENT-SPONSORED PLANS
DON'T BUILD OR PRESERVE WEALTH,
NOR DO THEY SAVE TAXES.

A deferred tax is nothing more than a compounded/larger tax at an uncertain tax rate in the future.

ELEVEN

TO ROTH OR NOT TO ROTH?

THE MOST SERIOUS MISTAKES ARE NOT BEING MADE AS A RESULT OF THE WRONG ANSWERS. THE TRUE DANGEROUS THING IS ASKING THE WRONG QUESTIONS.

—PETER DRUCKER

Part of immersing myself in the world of government-sponsored plans meant getting a grasp on the Roth IRA. Everyone asks me, "What do you think about the Roth?"

A Roth IRA is an individual retirement account to which you can contribute after-tax dollars. Your money then grows tax-free, and you can generally make tax-free and penalty-free withdrawals after age 59½. (You can withdraw earlier but not without stipulations.)

Conversely, with a traditional IRA, your contributions are made with pre-tax dollars. Your money then grows tax-deferred, and your withdrawals are taxed as current income after age 59½.

I think the reason people are so fascinated with the Roth is because it just seems like a better deal. But is it really? If you want to have some fun, the next time you meet with your tax professional, banker, or financial planner, ask them to show you the difference in outcomes between the Roth and the traditional IRA. And then see which one they recommend. Many will tell you that you should expect to be in a lower tax bracket when you retire. If that's the case, you may want to ask yourself, "How poor do I want to be when I retire?" Then, I'd begin searching for a new advisor.

To answer the question about which IRA is better, why don't we begin with a little experiment? Let's pair the two side by side and run some numbers. Now, I am aware that there are variables such as age, adjusted gross income, etc., that can come into play with these plans. But for this example, let's simply try to keep all things equal and get to the bottom line. Let's assume:

* You contributed $30,000 to both plans.
* You are in the 33% income tax bracket.
* You will also retire in the same 33% income tax bracket.
* You use the same investment portfolio and advisor for both plans with an investment rate of return of 7.2%.
* All variables remain the same: tax rate, growth rate, and withdrawal rate.

We'll illustrate the differences between these plans over a 10-year period and see which one outperforms the other. Using the traditional IRA (pre-tax) illustration, it should look like this:

IRA PRE-TAX

GROSS	$30,000
NO TAX TODAY	- $0
NET TO INVEST	$30,000

**$30,000 @ 7.2% FOR 10 YEARS
= $60,000**

**TAX-DEFERRED VALUE $60,000
ANNUAL INTEREST INCOME @ 7.2%
= $4,320**

Using the Roth (after-tax) illustration, it should look like this:

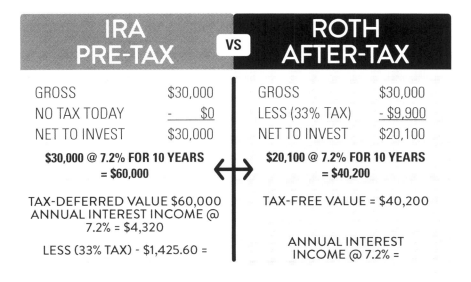

IRA PRE-TAX VS ROTH AFTER-TAX

IRA PRE-TAX		ROTH AFTER-TAX	
GROSS	$30,000	GROSS	$30,000
NO TAX TODAY	- $0	LESS (33% TAX)	- $9,900
NET TO INVEST	$30,000	NET TO INVEST	$20,100

**$30,000 @ 7.2% FOR 10 YEARS
= $60,000**   **$20,100 @ 7.2% FOR 10 YEARS
= $40,200**

TAX-DEFERRED VALUE $60,000
ANNUAL INTEREST INCOME @
7.2% = $4,320

TAX-FREE VALUE = $40,200

LESS (33% TAX) - $1,425.60 =

ANNUAL INTEREST
INCOME @ 7.2% =

And when we compare the two side by side, they look like this:

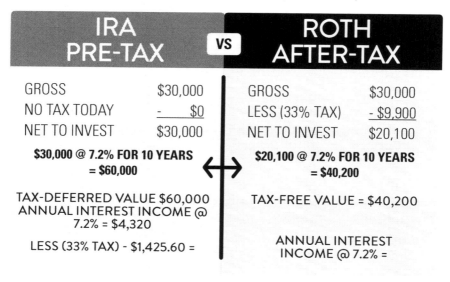

Now, let's look at the bottom line and see what we find:

SAME NET SPENDABLE INCOME!

Both plans come out with exactly the same net spendable income!

In truth, determining which plan is better depends on your objectives. Clearly, if you are in the same tax bracket at the start and finish and each plan experiences the same growth, there is no difference between the two. But if you expect to be in a higher tax bracket at retirement, the Roth appears to be a better option. Remember what we just covered in the last chapter? It's almost always smarter to pay the taxes on the seed than it is to wait and pay your taxes on the harvest.

However, the truth of the matter is that we may simply be asking the wrong question from the get-go. Instead of trying so hard to figure out which of these two IRA plans is the better option, perhaps there's an altogether different route that will yield an even better return than the road most traveled.

Between the two, I prefer the Roth. But, simply put, you'll never build true wealth with a government-sponsored plan, no matter when you pay the taxes. Real wealth comes from developing and understanding money from a much broader perspective, and that includes having a tax strategy. That's exactly where we are heading next.

Peak Performance Tip #11

The **NET SPENDABLE INCOME IS THE SAME** between a **ROTH** and a **TRADITIONAL IRA**, given tax rates and portfolio rates remain the same.

TWELVE

DEEP IN THE HEART OF TAXES

I JUST TAUGHT MY KIDS ABOUT TAXES
BY EATING 38% OF THEIR ICE CREAM.
—CONAN O'BRIEN

As my career unfolded, I came to understand that there is one topic everyone has to face—**TAXES**. Like it or not, taxes are part of life, and not all investments are taxed the same. For most Americans, taxes are something they approach with great disdain. However, for the wealthy-minded, they become a huge part of money management and financial and estate planning.

In case you don't believe how erosive taxes can be, let me tell you a story about an Indiana client of mine who worked for his employer for forty-seven years. Upon his retirement, they wanted to give him a bonus of $100,000 net of taxes. But later he received an email from the CFO of the company outlining the overall tax implications. You won't believe it! Here's the breakdown:

* Federal Tax: $32,800
* Social Security Tax: $6,570
* Medicare Tax: $2,151
* Indiana State Tax: $4,674
* Allen County Tax: $2,199

With all of the federal, state, and county taxes, plus Social Security and Medicare, his company actually had to give him $148,394 for him to get the full $100,000 bonus!

Hear me on this:

Over the course of our lifetime, I believe most Americans will pay more in taxes than they will ever save or invest for retirement.

Well-respected CPA Ed Slott recently told Forbes, "Taxes are the single biggest factor that separates us from our retirement dreams."[12]

He's right on the mark. Think about the national debt in this country. It currently sits at $35 trillion. In 2027, it's projected to reach over $46 trillion, with US unfunded liabilities at over $260 trillion. This results in liabilities per US citizen at $772,000.[13] It can be overwhelming to think about, as eventually, that bill is going to come due. To fund the interest payments, the government bill will exceed the Social Security and military bills combined!

So how will it get paid? Well, once again, let me ask: **Do you think future tax rates will go up, come down, or stay the same?** I think the answer is pretty obvious. In fact, in his book *Comeback America: Turning the Country Around and Restoring Fiscal Responsibility,* David Walker, formerly known as the nation's CPA (when he

"OVER THE COURSE OF OUR LIFETIME BELIEVE MOST AMERICANS WILL **PAY MORE IN TAXES THAN** THEY WILL *EVER* **SAVE OR INVEST** FOR **RETIREMENT**."

—PHIL BODINE

worked as the U.S. Comptroller General under Presidents George H. W. Bush and Bill Clinton), said that tax rates needed to double— if not triple—as the government tries to get its debt under control.

Just looking at the latest statistics gives us an indication of how it is beginning to play out. Some people feel that making the rich pay more in taxes is the solution. But how do we define "the rich?" Would it be all those "greedy" millionaires and billionaires? It may surprise you to know that:[14]

* If you earned $115,000 in 2022, you were in the top 10% of US wage earners.

* If you earned $165,000 in 2022, you were in the top 5% of US wage earners.

* If you earned $350,000 in 2022, you were in the top 1% of US wage earners.

* If you earned $500,000 in 2022, you were in the top 0.2% of US wage earners.

So, which category of rich people should we tax more heavily? In the meantime, the middle and lower-income sectors always seem to get hurt the worst, as you can see with the latest statistics regarding the number of Americans who paid no taxes:[15]

2020 59.3%

2021 56.0%

2022 40.1%

2023 40.1%

Suffice it to say, the tax train is coming, and the time to start planning is now while we're still in control.

So what does that mean? What does that look like?

"NOT ALL ASSETS ARE TAXED THE SAME."

—PHIL BODINE

When it comes to investing, we already talked about paying tax on the seed rather than the harvest. But that's only part of the equation. In the vast spectrum of financial planning, just about every advisor talks about the diversification of assets. Yet, I've never come across an advisor who speaks about the diversification of taxes. **Learning to plan and diversify the tax treatment of your income streams, both pre- and-post-retirement is CRUCIAL to the success or failure of your financial future.**

REMEMBER THIS:
Every financial decision you make today will either increase or decrease your retirement income.

—Phil Bodine

Take a look at our **Tax Control Quadrant®** below and notice that not all quadrants are taxed the same. There are four tax quadrants you can position money into:

❶ Tax-Deferred, Fully Taxable Income

❷ Partial/Ordinary Taxable Income

❸ Tax-Free Income

❹ Tax-Exempt Income

TAX CONTROL QUADRANT®

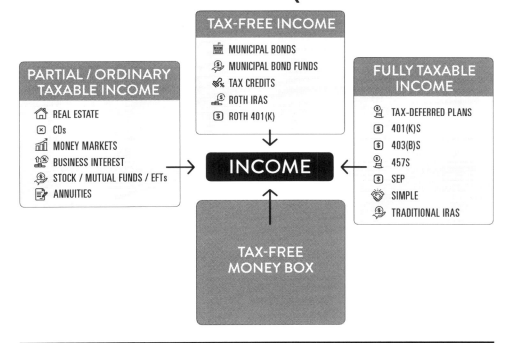

TAX-FREE INCOME
- MUNICIPAL BONDS
- MUNICIPAL BOND FUNDS
- TAX CREDITS
- ROTH IRAS
- ROTH 401(K)

PARTIAL / ORDINARY TAXABLE INCOME
- REAL ESTATE
- CDs
- MONEY MARKETS
- BUSINESS INTEREST
- STOCK / MUTUAL FUNDS / EFTs
- ANNUITIES

FULLY TAXABLE INCOME
- TAX-DEFERRED PLANS
- 401(K)S
- 403(B)S
- 457S
- SEP
- SIMPLE
- TRADITIONAL IRAS

INCOME

TAX-FREE MONEY BOX

THE GOAL:
MONEY WITH TAX CONTROL PRE- AND POST-RETIREMENT

"WHAT IS YOUR STRATEGY TO INSULATE YOUR WEALTH FROM TAXES?"

—PHIL BODINE

FULLY TAXABLE INCOME

Let's begin with fully taxable income assets. This includes tax-deferred retirement products such as 401(k)s, 403(b)s, 457s, SEPs, SIMPLE, tax-sheltered annuities, and traditional IRAs—the government-sponsored plans I discussed earlier.

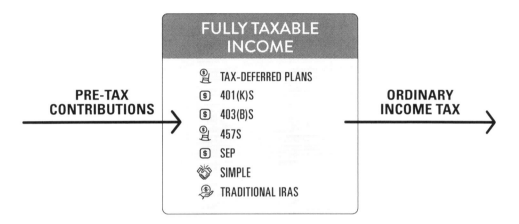

As you now know, and I wish to reiterate, government-sponsored plans never end well. Qualified plans feel good at the beginning, but they are taxed as ordinary income when you withdraw. **They are great accumulators but bad distributors**.

These plans will end up being your worst wealth-building assets—every time. That's because the money isn't yours. It belongs to the government, and it's locked up. There has never been any sustainable wealth created in our country with government-sponsored plans.

PARTIAL/ORDINARY TAXABLE INCOME

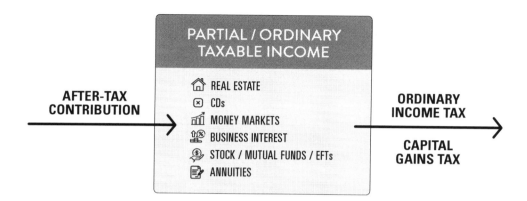

This quadrant is considered a partial tax category and includes investments like real estate, CDs, money markets, business interest, mutual funds, options, annuities, and equities. These are the types of products that can help offset tax liabilities due to capital gains transactions. As a side note, the tax code in its current form today was written with the small business owner in mind.

Running your own business can prove to be one of the best options for implementing effective tax strategies. I've always said, "Other than yourself, your business is always your best investment. In my opinion, no other advisor can show you a better investment than your own business. The second best investment is real estate."

TAX-FREE INCOME

This is the quadrant that includes municipal bonds, municipal bond funds, tax credits, and Roth IRAs, and allows us to take advantage of tax-free income. You may be wondering, "What is tax-free income?"

That's a great question. In fact, if you want to have some fun, see if your accountant knows the difference between "tax-free" and "tax-exempt" income. Many do not.

Allow me to explain. While the above Municipal Bonds and Roth IRAs are all designated as tax-free income, they are still considered **reportable income on your tax return,** and they may work against you when it comes to Medicare, Medicaid, and Social Security taxation. You don't pay tax on reportable income; it is tax-free but not tax-exempt. That brings us to the fourth quadrant.

TAX-EXEMPT INCOME

Income is only tax-exempt if you're not required to report it on your tax return. To my knowledge, there are only half a dozen places in the tax code that use the terminology "tax-exempt." The tax-exempt quadrant is one most people never discover. And if they do, they seldom understand how to make it work in their favor.

I know what you're thinking. "Is there really a financial product or vehicle that will allow people to avoid paying taxes? That sounds too good to be true."

Well, let me ask you this: If there were such a vehicle, what percentage of your assets would you want to have with no risk and be off the radar screen of the IRS? I've asked this question a thousand times, and most people respond somewhere between 50% to 100% of their overall assets.

But first things first. Is it even possible? Is it even legally, ethically, and morally allowed?

Yes, yes, and yes!

The vehicle I'm referring to is what I like to call **THE SOLUTION**—the device that ties everything together. The reason most people never achieve true wealth is that they don't really understand the significance of tax diversification and how to employ, what I like to call a **"tax-free money box,"** to help them reach their financial objectives. The good news for you is that I'm about to explain exactly how it's done.

Peak Performance Tip #12

Tax diversification is just as important as asset or investment diversification.

Remember, **NOT ALL MONEY IS TAXED THE SAME**.

OLDER AND **WISER** ...

RISK MITIGATION:
HOPE FOR THE BEST,
BUT PLAN FOR THE WORST.

THIRTEEN

THE FOUNDATION OF PROTECTION

ALWAYS GO TO OTHER PEOPLE'S FUNERALS;
OTHERWISE THEY WON'T COME TO YOURS.

—YOGI BERRA

Well, we've covered a lot of ground so far. We've debunked myths regarding banks, financial entertainers, and compound interest. We've addressed misconceptions about average rate of return, term life insurance, and mortgage debt. We've even exposed the truth about insurance deductibles, government-sponsored retirement plans, and taxes.

But what I'm about to share with you is something you'll never hear from 99% of the advisors in the industry. It's what I've termed "The Solution" to the problems covered in Chapters 1–12.

With close to four decades of personal business experience as an advisor, I've discovered there's actually a solution that can tackle

166 | *Phil Bodine*

every one of the financial challenges presented in this book, which we'll cover in the next three chapters. I can tell you that it's better than anything else you'll find in the mainstream market today.

I'm not talking about a pie-in-the-sky, get-rich-quick scheme or some risky, far-fetched idea that will cause others to question your sanity. Believe it or not, every topic we've covered can be addressed through one specific, properly structured entity.

The financial instrument I'm talking about is more reliable than any bank or stock investment. It allows you to put your money into an account and reap a guaranteed annual rate of return. In fact, you can borrow against your account and pay it back **WHEN** you want, **HOW** you want, or even **IF** you want, and it won't impact the equity growth you had in your account, nor affect your credit score as it is a private loan. I should also mention that it's tax-exempt, and it's guaranteed to give the entire accumulated balance to your family when you pass away tax-free!

Let me ask you this **IMPORTANT** question.

How quickly can you turn your assets into cash without doing two things:

❶ triggering a tax,

❷ reducing the growth or earnings potential?

The financial tool I am talking about is a whole life insurance contract. But it's not just any life insurance contract. It's a properly structured contract specifically designed to operate as a tax-free, flow-through vehicle for all your financial undertakings. A house is only as good as its foundation, and the foundation of your financial plan will determine how far you will go in life.

The reason you won't hear about this strategy from other advisors is because:

❶ They are unaware of them because they lack the education.

❷ They don't know how they work.

❸ They don't know how to construct or design them properly to work to your advantage.

In all honesty, most insurance advisors who sell life insurance policies do so with a strong focus on the death benefit, but that's not our sole primary objective.

I'm well aware that almost everyone considers life insurance a four-letter word. I've seen people roll their eyes, shut notebooks, and tune me out during my financial workshops right after the words "life insurance" come out of my mouth. I want to encourage you to stay with me as I explain. It reminds me of the wise old saying, "Great minds are like parachutes. They work better if you keep them open."

Wade D. Pfau, Ph.D., CFA®,[16] RICP®, and a professor of retirement income planning at the American College of Financial Planning, proclaimed the following, "The financial services profession is generally divided between two camps: those focusing on investment solutions and those focusing on insurance solutions. **My research shows that the most efficient retirement strategies require an integration of BOTH investments and insurance."**[17] In other words, when combined, you have a more consistent, predictable, and productive outcome.

Most people simply don't understand life insurance. In fact, when I first came into this business in 1989, I didn't understand it, either. All I wanted to do was manage money, not promote life insurance. However, I learned quickly that when it comes to money, ignorance isn't bliss—it's expensive. And I couldn't afford to be ignorant for my clients.

I cut my teeth in the financial world by working alongside a man named Roger Summers, who has all the financial credentials—JD, CFP®, CLU®, ChFC®. Let's just say he is well-educated. He used to drive me crazy because every single one of his client meetings included a conversation about life insurance. This led to many endless debates between the two of us.

Roger would argue that life insurance always fits because you're buying your net worth. You are essentially purchasing future dollars at a discount for pennies on the dollar. Then he would talk, ad nauseam, about the tax ramifications, multiplying wealth, liquidity, and how there is more certainty in life insurance than there is in buying and selling stocks. I wasn't convinced, but I did respect him. So I listened.

Then, in 1992, I went to a three-day financial symposium in Chicago, where I heard a presentation by an economist named Robert Castiglione. Robert began by talking about how compound interest is a losing strategy. This was back when certificates of deposits (CDs) paid approximately 9%. I sat there thinking, "There's no way compounding your money is a losing strategy."

Then Robert proved it—mathematically. He explained that as your money compounds, so do your taxes. And so does your lost opportunity cost because you're paying more taxes. And in the end, it doesn't work as promised.

Castiglione re-introduced me to economic principles I learned in college but had never applied. One was called "economic wealth eroding factors of money," and it included things like taxes, inflation, market fluctuations, risk, lost opportunity costs, technological change, planned obsolescence, tax law changes, consumer financing, fees, and unexpected life events. He taught me that no matter how hard you swim from point A to point B in the ocean, the water current is always a factor, and it can change on any given day. When it comes to finances, many people unknowingly fall prey to these wealth-eroding factors and economic threats. Yet, there is a way to prevent them from destroying investments.

Sitting there listening to Castiglione, I realized I had never looked at money this way. I found myself becoming more and more fascinated and mesmerized with every word that came out of his mouth. And then he revealed the saving grace to the eroding factors. It was, of course, the thing I despised most—life insurance.

Several months later, I convinced Roger Summers to join me at a financial advisor forum in Scottsdale, Arizona, where Castiglione was scheduled to speak again. I really wanted Roger's expert opinion on what he had to say.

It didn't take long. During the first break, Roger leaned over to me and said, "Everything this guy is saying is 100% spot-on. He is telling the truth. He knows, from an economic standpoint, how money really works. I would encourage you to invest all your time and resources into what he is teaching."

I spent the next seven years and over $100,000 training myself to learn everything possible about using **life insurance as the cornerstone of financial planning**.

What I discovered was that, despite the preconceived notions most people have about this vehicle, a properly designed cash flow life insurance contract, when used correctly, can absolutely revolutionize wealth management! It can be used as a foundation for protection, a wealth optimizer (see Chapter 2), a productive savings tool, a tax-free, flow-through entity, a corporate financing tool, and a structure that includes every component of an ideal financial plan. **It's like owning a Financial Swiss Army Knife! (For all 70 benefits, see Appendix Two at the back of the book.)**

CASH FLOW LIFE INSURANCE

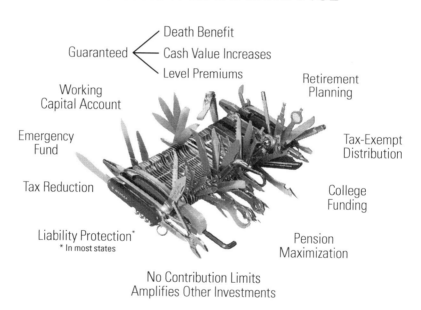

Guaranteed ⟨ Death Benefit / Cash Value Increases / Level Premiums

Working Capital Account

Emergency Fund

Tax Reduction

Liability Protection*
* In most states

Retirement Planning

Tax-Exempt Distribution

College Funding

Pension Maximization

No Contribution Limits
Amplifies Other Investments

THE FINANCIAL SWISS ARMY KNIFE

A properly structured cash flow life insurance contract is so multifaceted that I'm devoting the next chapter to explaining its benefits, those most people don't even know exist. Also called permanent life insurance, this vehicle is a game-changer used by the majority of prudent wealthy people and all of the mainstream banks. It's also one of the best-kept secrets in the financial world. For the first time, I understood how to leverage an underutilized financial loophole that America's wealthiest families use to build and storehouse wealth.

Consider the Rockefeller family. What do you think is the secret to the Rockefellers' rise to wealth and power? This family got their start with John D. Rockefeller in the oil industry in 1863 by investing in a Cleveland, Ohio refinery. In 1870, he established **Standard Oil**, which eventually controlled around **90%** of U.S. refineries and pipelines by the early 1880s, but they have stayed rich and powerful for seven generations thanks to a special strategy called "The Rockefeller Waterfall Method." On the other hand, the Vanderbilts, who were once even richer, lost their wealth by the fourth generation.

What is the Waterfall Method that has made all the difference for the Rockefellers? Every single Rockefeller family member gets a very large life insurance policy put on them at birth. The money from these policies goes into a family trust, and then inside the trust, there is a cash-value life insurance policy that works like a family bank. As the family bank is inside the trust, it acts like a family vault. All the family members can take loans from it, and as they do this, generation after generation, the trust keeps growing, therefore making the family richer and more powerful, thus creating generational wealth.

Life insurance increases the stability of the business world, raises its moral tone, and puts a premium upon those habits of thrift and saving, which are so essential to the welfare of the people as a body.

—Theodore Roosevelt, U.S. President (1901–1909)

That's what we mean by Wealth in Overdrive®—ours is a customized strategy designed to accelerate wealth with more efficiency, added protection, and lower risk, while paying fewer taxes. **This strategy isn't just for the wealthiest but for you as well!**

As a comprehensive wealth advisor, it's not my job to get clients from Point A to Point B. Most of them can do that on their own. My job is to help them get from Point C to Point Z with no out-of-pocket costs, less risk, and fewer taxes while still reaching their destination. That includes teaching them to see things differently than the rest of the crowd.

All that aside, I'm well aware that even mentioning the words "life insurance" can stop a conversation in an instant. So, in the next chapter, we'll address the elephant in the room head-on so we can position *your wealth into overdrive.*

For a more comprehensive understanding of the benefits of whole life insurance, I invite you to watch a short video I put together to better inform my clients. To watch **"10-Minute Lesson on Life Insurance,"** simply scan the QR code below and take a listen.

Peak Performance Tip #13

Great minds are like parachutes.
They work better if you **keep** them **open**.

"WEALTH IN OVERDRIVE® IS A CUSTOMIZED **STRATEGY** DESIGNED TO **ACCELERATE WEALTH** WITH MORE EFFICIENCY, ADDED **PROTECTION,** AND **LOWER RISK,** WHILE **PAYING FEWER TAXES**."

—PHIL BODINE

"No, I can't be bothered to hear about some bright idea . . .
I have a battle to fight!"

FOURTEEN

PERCEPTION VS. REALITY

IT AIN'T WHAT YOU DON'T KNOW THAT GETS YOU INTO TROUBLE. IT'S WHAT YOU KNOW FOR SURE THAT JUST AIN'T SO.

—MARK TWAIN

When I was a kid, I loved to go swimming during the summertime. One of the things my parents always told me was to "wait an hour after eating before getting back into the pool to avoid cramping." This was the common mantra of all parents at the time. Perhaps it still is today.

The problem is, nothing about this quote is true. Eating a normal-sized meal before swimming has never been proven to cause cramping. Yet it's such a widely known expression that it's automatically believed to be gospel truth. We live in a world full of such catchphrases. For example, how many of these slogans are you familiar with?

* We only use 10% of our brains.
* George Washington had wooden teeth.
* It takes seven years for your body to digest gum.
* The Great Wall of China can be seen from outer space.
* Touching a toad will give you warts.
* Bats are blind.
* Lightning never strikes twice in the same place.
* Shaving will make your hair grow back thicker.
* Breakfast is the most important meal of the day.
* Cracking your knuckles causes arthritis.
* Sugar makes children hyper.

These sayings are so embedded in our culture that they are rarely ever questioned. Yet none of them are true. And in the financial world, you'd be hard-pressed to find a topic more encompassed with mythical remarks than insurance. My observation is that most people hate life insurance. Any argument? However, everybody needs life insurance but no one wants it because they don't understand how it works. Or if they do have it, they have the wrong type or the wrong structure.

Based on my experience, I have found ten primary reasons to be true about why people are skeptical about permanent life insurance. This is a problem because they prevent people from even looking at this invaluable opportunity before them. Let's take a look at each of them, and hopefully, by the end of this chapter, you can feel more confident about adding this financial tool to your toolbox.

10 REASONS PEOPLE ARE SKEPTICAL ABOUT PERMANENT LIFE INSURANCE

REASON #1: Perception

Many people look at life insurance as a scam. It's a product nobody wants to talk about, much less purchase. Since age and health factor into the price, policies can seem like a waste of time and money. Besides, who wants to make never-ending payments for a product that just sits in a bank deposit box collecting dust and goes to someone else at your death? And since the death benefit is the main focus, it's no wonder perception is the #1 reason people despise life insurance.

I realize it takes a major paradigm shift for people to sit down and objectively look at life insurance as a productive, life-giving financial tool rather than simply as a product. Even big financial firms don't seem to grasp the benefits because of perception. A co-worker of mine, who previously worked for a nationally known full-service broker-dealer company (often referred to as a "wire-house" company), told me that they never touched life insurance because it didn't do much in the way of making any money for the firm. Plus, it was a lot more exciting to talk about assets under management like stocks, bonds, cash, gold, and pie charts than it was something as boring as life insurance.

However, I've found that if you want to pursue real wealth beyond the common life, it's vital to look at life insurance beyond the common perception. What if life insurance were free? What if there were five ways to spend the death benefit while you were still alive? First of all, how much would you want? And would that change your perception?

REASON #2: No Need

I understand that nobody wants life insurance. And there may even be some instances where you feel like you don't "need" life insurance. I hear it all the time: "I don't need it."

But if you have either of these thoughts going through your head, it may be an indication that you, too, are still looking at life insurance as strictly a product with a death benefit.

In 2014, Forbes published an article titled "Mystery Billionaire Buys Record-Breaking $201 Million Life Insurance Contract"! The article stated that the purchaser was an unidentified Silicon Valley tech investor who, at the time of the purchase, set the Guinness World Record for the Most Valuable Life Insurance Contract. The deal involved nineteen different insurance companies![18] Why in the world would a billionaire purchase such a product? If anyone doesn't "need" life insurance, it would be a billionaire, right? What does this mystery man know that others don't? Well, he knows enough to understand that life insurance is about more than just a death benefit.

When former Michigan football head coach Jim Harbaugh negotiated his $7 million per year contract with the Wolverines, he structured it with life insurance. Essentially, Michigan funded Harbaugh's salary increase by paying a $2 million annual premium for seven years through the end of the coach's contract in December 2021. It's estimated that, based on that $2 million annual premium, after they pay the expense of his plan back to the university at his death, there could be at least $20 million left, tax-free, for his wife, his kids, and his trust. The split-dollar plan will support him in retirement (tax-exempt), pay back the school, and leave his family a large amount of completely tax-free wealth. Harbaugh can withdraw or take loans against it free of tax or penalty at any time.

This is a savvy tax strategy. Did he "need" it? Probably not. But he and his advisors understood its potential and the freedom it offered him.

Another example of this would be husband and wife clients of mine who both graduated from Harvard. They went on to work for a little company called Bain Capital, and when they eventually retired (at the ripe old age of thirty-eight), they couldn't figure out what to do with their $36 million portfolio. They had no kids. In fact, they had no plans of ever having any children. They were completely happy with their four dogs. And they weren't particularly charitably-minded. So when I asked the husband what he wanted to do with all his money, he simply replied, "Make more."

When I noticed they were putting $25,000 a year into a little Mass-Mutual whole life insurance contract, I asked him, "Why so little?"

He responded, "Well, I don't need it."

When I showed him how he could use his life insurance as a tax-free flow-through entity and a vehicle to grow his portfolio and make it more tax-efficient, it was like a light switch went on inside his head. He now deposits over $1 million annually into their life insurance portfolio. Trust me, this couple doesn't really "need" more life insurance. But they understand that it isn't just strictly about the death benefit. It is about using it as a non-correlated financial asset on their road to true wealth.

REASON #3: Cost

People sometimes look at whole life insurance and decide it's too expensive. Compared to the term life insurance policies that many financial entertainers are promoting, I can see why they would feel that way. But we've already covered why term insurance isn't the key to your long-term financial success. So, let's take a closer look at a properly structured whole life contract by comparing it to a certificate of deposit.

If you deposit $25,000/year for 20 years into a whole life insurance contract vs. the same deposit going into a CD paying 5%, there's essentially no cost to the life insurance, whether you live or die.

RETIREMENT INCOME
DETERMINED BY ACCUMULATION **AND** DISTRIBUTION RATE

AGE	ANNUAL DEPOSIT	RETIREMENT INCOME	ACCUMULATED EQUITY	LIFE INSURANCE	CD @ 5% (35% TAX RATE)
46	$25,000				
47	$25,000				
48	$25,000				
49	$25,000				
50	$25,000				
51	$25,000				
52	$25,000				
53	$25,000				
54	$25,000				
55	$25,000		$274,094	$911,578	$299,341
56	$25,000				
57	$25,000				
58	$25,000				
59	$25,000				
60	$25,000				
61	$25,000				
62	$25,000				
63	$25,000				
64	$25,000				
65	$25,000		$734,683	$1,365,226	$711,502

(10 years → 55)
(20 years → 65)

After ten years, the investment in the CD is slightly higher than the equity of the life insurance contract. However, the CD doesn't have a $911,000 tax-exempt death benefit. After twenty years, the CD value is $711,502. And after the contract is paid up, there are multiple ways to take out $50,000—tax-exempt—every single year until age ninety, equaling over $750,000 more than you deposited and still have over $555,000 tax-free death benefit.

THERE IS NO COST!

On the other hand, if you wanted to withdraw $50,000 from the CD, you'd run out of money by age eighty-three. How can life insurance outspend the CD? Because you have the ability to borrow the money **against** the contract while keeping your money at work earning interest and dividends without incurring a tax. It is considered a leveraged asset, just like real estate.

RETIREMENT INCOME
DETERMINED BY ACCUMULATION **AND** DISTRIBUTION RATE

AGE	ANNUAL DEPOSIT	RETIREMENT INCOME	ACCUMULATED EQUITY	LIFE INSURANCE	CD @ 5% (35% TAX RATE)
66	PAID UP	$50,000			
67	$0	$50,000			
68	$0	$50,000			
69	$0	$50,000			
70	$0	$50,000			
71	$0	$50,000			
72	$0	$50,000			
73	$0	$50,000			
74	$0	$50,000			
75	$0	$50,000	$559,774	$1,106,697	$380,981
76	$0	$50,000			
77	$0	$50,000			
78	$0	$50,000			
79	$0	$50,000			
80	$0	$50,000			
81	$0	$50,000			
82	$0	$50,000			
83	$0	$50,000			$28,907
84	$0	$50,000			$0 ← Out of money!
85	$0	$50,000	$326,300	$750,174	$0
86	$0	$50,000			$0
87	$0	$50,000			$0
88	$0	$50,000			$0
89	$0	$50,000			$0
90	$0	$50,000	$184,405	$555,721	$0
TOTALS	$500,000	$1,250,000			

With a properly designed contract, you can borrow money against your equity in the policy. The beautiful thing is that it never disrupts the exponential growth of the wealth optimizer curve, as referred to

"LIFE INSURANCE ISN'T THE BEST ACCUMULATOR OF **WEALTH**; IT'S A BETTER **DISTRIBUTOR** AND **PRESERVER OF WEALTH**."

–PHIL BODINE

in Chapter 2. Both the cash value and the equity value continue to grow uninterrupted. This is true whether you pay the loan back or not. And the best part is that you aren't paying taxes on the money you borrow against your contract because it's a private, non-recourse loan, and it doesn't show up on a credit report. You are able to turn your life insurance asset into cash without triggering any taxes or any disruption in the compounded growth of the equity. That's the miracle of an uninterrupted exponential growth curve working for you and not against you! (See Wealth Optimizer graphic on page 56.)

It's not quite as easy to do this with your CD investment. You would actually need $75,000 per year of income from a taxable investment to equal the $50,000 per year tax-free income from your life insurance contract.

At a safe withdrawal rate of 3.5%, you would need over $2.14 million in investments to produce $75,000 per year of income! In order to accumulate $2.14 million in investments from ages 45 to 65 while saving $25,000 per year, you would need a guaranteed **capital equivalent value rate of return of 12.99%** each and every year! And that's a pretty tall order. The definition of **capital equivalent value rate of return** is what other investment opportunities would have to earn as a rate of return in order to provide the same monetary benefits as a difficult-to-value competing investment or life insurance contract.

Life insurance isn't the best accumulator of wealth; it's a better distributor and preserver of wealth.

Having life insurance will actually increase the value of your wealth portfolio and your estate. So, as I mentioned, there really is no cost but many benefits. As Warren Buffet stated, **"Price is what you pay. Value is what you get."**

REASON #4: High Commissions

Insurance agents are a dime a dozen. In the minds of the public, they seem to come and go as quickly as used car salesmen. And it's hard to take them too seriously if you feel they are lining their pockets with a big commission when they sell you a contract. But in reality, the amount of compensation an advisor makes is determined by the design of the contract.

I have a friend who retired and sold his partnership shares in a large insurance business. He had been in the insurance business for forty-two years. I was honored to get his call, asking me to design a life insurance contract for him to provide additional protection and enhance his portfolio. Even though he was excited that I agreed to put together a better contract for him, he gave me a hard time about all the commission he'd be paying me.

So, I told him not to worry since his insurance license was still active, and I'd give him my compensation. And that's exactly what I did. The day I received my first check, I waited until he was in town and personally handed it to him. He looked at it, glanced back up at me, and exclaimed, "That's all?" I reminded him that I had done what I promised I would do.

The compensation paid on an insurance contract almost always comes down to the design or the structure. Policies can be shaped to reduce compensation for the advisor by as much as 80% less than typical payouts. That's why I stress that a **properly designed** whole life contract can be constructed for maximum benefit. **Keep in mind that over 90% of the designs I come across in the marketplace are plans I would never want to own myself.**

REASON #5: Bad Investment

When people tell me that insurance is a bad investment, I typically respond, **"Bad investment compared to what? Stocks? Bonds? Real Estate?"**

When I was twenty-nine years old, I took out an insurance contract and deposited $10,000 into it every year. Now, thirty years later, the cash value of that contract is more than three times what I put into it—**Net, Net, Net!** Essentially, I'm getting four dollars for every dollar I put into the contract—all tax-exempt. Is that a good deal? **YES!**

My internal tax-free rate of return was an amazing 6%. To net that same 6% rate of return externally means I would have to account for the taxes. In other words, I'd need to reap an even higher return on my investments to net a 6% gain . . . **NET, NET, NET** . . . net of fees, net of lost opportunity cost, net of taxes, and all at no risk!

For example, if I were in the 15% tax bracket and wanted to have a 6% net gain on my investments, my investments would have to pull 7.05%.

If I were in the 25% tax bracket, my external investments would need to be at 8%.

What I'm saying is that the higher the tax bracket you are in, the better your investments must do to achieve the same simple 6% tax-free result of having your money grow internally within a contract. Take a look:

TAX EQUIVALENT RATE OF RETURN

TAX-FREE ROR = 6.00%	
FEDERAL TAX BRACKET	**TAXABLE RATE OF RETURN**
15.0%	7.05%
25.0%	8.00%
28.0%	8.34%
33.0%	9.00%
35.0%	9.23%
37.0%	9.53%
39.6%	9.95%

* DOES NOT INCLUDE STATE INCOME TAXES

If you feel you can do better with a particular investment, you do have the option to simply reinvest the equity of your contract any way you want. In fact, my wife and I bought all of our rental real estate **through** our life insurance policies.

Does that mean that life insurance is a better investment than real estate? No, it doesn't. Life insurance has benefits that are similar to real estate, but there are some differences. Take a look:

🏠 REAL ESTATE	VS	🛡 LIFE INSURANCE
⊠ TAXABLE		⊘ TAX-EXEMPT
⊠ MAINTENANCE		⊘ NO MAINTENANCE
⊠ PROPERTY TAXES		⊘ NO PROPERTY TAXES
⊠ PROPERTY INSURANCE		⊘ NO PROPERTY INSURANCE
⊠ TENANTS		⊘ NO TENANTS
⊠ NOT GUARANTEED		⊘ GUARANTEED
⊠ NOT LIQUID		⊘ LIQUID

With property, you either pay for it all yourself or borrow it from the bank and pay it back with interest (determined by the bank). With life insurance, you can design a plan that works best for you. You have no property taxes. You have no maintenance. You have no obligations. With life insurance, you avoid the three T's—no Tenants, no Toilets, and no Taxes.

THE IRS TAX CODE INTERPRETS LIFE INSURANCE AS REAL PROPERTY

Stemming from a 1911 court case, Grigsby v. Russell, 222 U.S. 149, the Supreme Court held that the policy owner has the right to transfer an insurance policy. The Supreme Court opined that since life insurance had all the basic characteristics of property, it qualified as an asset that the policy owner could transfer without any limitations. The court drew a parallel between the ownership right in a life insurance policy and ownership rights in investment assets like stocks and bonds. Today, life insurance policy owners enjoy such rights as:

* the right to name a life insurance beneficiary;
* the right to change the beneficiary designation;
* the right to assign the policy;
* the right to borrow against a policy; and,
* the right to sell the policy to another party.

In Section 731.a.2, this code governs taxation for distributions from a partnership to a partner. It says that a distribution of property, other than cash and marketable securities, from the partnership, is not a taxable event. This is usually the code section we are referencing when we say that life insurance is "taxed as property" because, under the code section, it is not taxed as cash or securities.

Don't get me wrong! I'm not saying you should sink all your money into life insurance. That's not what this book is about. But life insurance is a foundation of protection and a permission slip that allows you to use it as a tax-free, flow-through entity to invest in other things like real estate, stocks, or whatever your heart desires. Wise investors should be embracing life insurance as a separate integral asset class in and of itself instead of disengaging and completely ignoring it.

Life insurance is a solution to a problem that exists. IT IS NOT AN ENGINE! The investment is an engine, and life insurance is the turbocharger that makes the engine more efficient. It doesn't drive the financial plan itself. That would be the stocks, bonds, real estate retirement plans, and other investments. **Again, life insurance isn't a good accumulator of wealth; it's a better distributor and preserver of wealth.**

What do these four pictures all have in common?

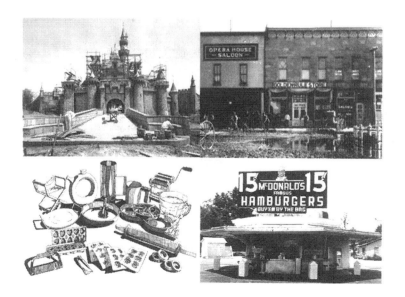

"WHAT'S THE **RATE OF RETURN** ON WALT DISNEY'S **LIFE INSURANCE CONTRACT**?"

—PHIL BODINE

The founders of these companies—Disneyland, McDonald's, JCPenney, and Pampered Chef—each borrowed against their life insurance policies to fund their businesses in the early days.

In **Walt Disney's** autobiography, he mentions that he borrowed $100,000 against his life insurance contract to start Disneyland. Because Disney had access to capital, he was able to borrow the money he needed when no one would loan him money for what is now the most famous theme park of all time. My question is this: **"What's the rate of return on Walt Disney's life insurance contract?"** The rate of return on his contract is incalculable, somewhere in the millions of percent.

Ray Kroc borrowed money against two of his cash-value life insurance policies to buy out the McDonald brothers in 1961, cover the salaries of key employees, and create an advertising campaign around the company's emerging mascot, Ronald McDonald.

J. C. Penney used his cash-value life insurance contract to keep his company afloat after the stock market crashed in 1929 and the ensuing Great Depression devastated U.S. department stores (along with his personal wealth). Penney borrowed against his contract to help his company meet its payroll and cover day-to-day expenses. This allowed the company to stay afloat and eventually rebound.

In 1980, **Doris Christopher** founded The Pampered Chef with $3,000 that she borrowed against her life insurance contract. Twenty-two years later, in 2002, Warren Buffett's Berkshire Hathaway paid approximately $1.2 billion to buy her company. Again, what was the rate of return on Doris Christopher's life insurance contract?

You may not have aspirations to start a theme park or a hamburger business. But you can learn to utilize life insurance as a vehicle to generate wealth in ways you never imagined. Using life insurance in this way is anything but a bad investment.

REASON #6: Media Misinformation

I've already touched on the impact that financial entertainers have on the general public. Their disservice is even more pronounced when it comes to their personal opinions on life insurance.

One website of a very famous financial "guru" incorrectly claims that term—not whole—life insurance is the key to future stability.

Another one claims that term life insurance is the way to go because it's the simplest. Both couldn't be more wrong! The reason many people don't understand the benefits of whole life insurance is partly due to unregistered and unqualified "entertainers" giving their generic personal opinions instead of their subjective professional opinions. They may not have any real tried-and-true experience, but they do have a platform! And they are tremendous marketers who can say pretty much whatever they want, never mind the fact that they aren't licensed or registered financial professionals. I'm sure they mean well, and they probably make a positive impact when it comes to helping people get out of debt or plan a budget. But when it comes to pursuing true wealth, these are not the people you want to be following.

Instead, look to people like Ed Slott, a CPA named the best source for IRA advice by *The Wall Street Journal*. He was the past Chairman of the New York State Society of CPAs Estate Planning Committee and editor of the IRA planning section of *The CPA Journal*. On the topic of life insurance, he says, **"The single biggest benefit in the federal tax code is the income-tax exemption for life**

"THE SINGLE **BIGGEST BENEFIT** IN THE FEDERAL TAX CODE IS THE INCOME-TAX **EXEMPTION FOR LIFE INSURANCE**."

"LIFE INSURANCE **SHOULD BE THE BEDROCK** OF ANY SERIOUS FINANCIAL, **RETIREMENT**, OR **ESTATE PLAN**."

— ED SLOTT, CPA
"BEST SOURCE OF IRA ADVICE"
—THE WALL STREET JOURNAL

insurance."[19] He also stated, "Life insurance should be the bedrock of any serious financial, retirement, or estate plan."[20]

When it comes to sound investing, I'll trust the professional opinions taught by credentialed experts over the personal opinions of unlicensed, unregistered financial entertainers any day.

REASON #7: Lack of Understanding

Life insurance uses terminology that may sound familiar but seldom used in everyday conversations. Words like "beneficiary," "deductible," "exclusions," "premium," "annuitant," "conversion," "face amount," and "nonforfeiture options" can sometimes even confuse the experts in the field. As a result, most people know just enough to be dangerous.

The truth is there is a huge lack of understanding with regard to how insurance works. In other words, insurance can be rather confusing with all its moving parts, and as they say, "a confused customer never buys."

REASON #8: Fear of the Unknown

Stepping outside of society's norms often involves fear of the unknown. Using a life insurance contract as a vehicle to improve your investments is not a whacked-out theory for people on the fringe, but it is outside the norm. And it takes a little courage to pursue this route. However, the more you investigate, the more you will find that this tool is used by the most astute investors in the world.

Don't let your fear of the unknown keep you from making wise decisions—especially when it comes to your money.

REASON #9: Misrepresentation

Over 90% of the insurance policies I come across are designed so poorly that I personally would never own any of them. And many insurance advisors have no idea what they are really selling. As a result, products get misrepresented all the time. This doesn't bode well for the insurance company, the advisor, or the customer, and it gives the industry a bad name.

REASON #10: Too Good to Be True

If you really delve into the many facets of life insurance and truly grasp the generally unknown benefits, you may find yourself thinking, "This sounds too good to be true. Why hasn't my advisor brought this to my attention? How come I didn't know any of this before?" I can't speak to that.

Take the example of Nobel Prize winner Albert Szent-Gyorgyi, a Hungarian Biochemist who discovered ascorbic acid, also known as Vitamin C, a common vitamin our bodies need that enables them to use carbohydrates, fats, and proteins efficiently. His discovery was among the foundations of modern nutrition. He said,

"Discovery consists of seeing what everybody has seen and thinking what nobody has thought."

I think this quote encapsulates the essence of true innovation, highlighting the importance of perceiving the world beyond surface-level observations and challenging conventional wisdom.

PERMANENT LIFE INSURANCE IS ALSO A COMMON TOOL USED IN UNCOMMON WAYS. The long history of preconceived notions surrounding insurance prevents most people from ever exploring or realizing the opportunity in front of them. And so, yes, it does come across as too good to be true, like it can't be real. But I assure you, it is!

SO, WHAT ABOUT THE 5-WAY TEST?

How does a properly designed whole life insurance contract stack up against the 5-Way Test that I use when making financial decisions? Let's find out.

1. Is it LIQUID? YES.

Do you remember Andi, the doctor I mentioned earlier in the book who worked with me to leverage her debt and create another income stream? She did this by taking out a life insurance contract. She then borrowed against that contract and used the funds to purchase that fancy, expensive medical laser that allowed her to expand her practice. Because she was simply borrowing against the contract vs. withdrawing, she continued to receive dividends and interest based on the high balance.

Compare this to trying to borrow money from your home, a government-sponsored plan, or the bank. It won't be easy or cheap, incurring fees, penalties, and taxes. With a properly designed life insurance contract, you can borrow against your plan over and over again, repaying yourself on your own terms—**when** you want, **how** you want, or **if** you want. It's considered a private, non-recourse loan and won't appear on a credit report. A life insurance contract can serve as a storehouse of assets to allow your money to be readily available. Now *that's* liquid.

2. Does it offer SAFETY? YES.

Life insurance companies are well-capitalized and highly regulated. They don't fail. They will make good on the contract because your policy is considered a **CONTRACT**, not an investment. If it were an investment, it would be taxed.

Look at what happened with the economic and financial chaos caused by COVID-19. While many people in the country panicked about their investments, clients of mine simply watched the value of their policies rise every day. When your funds are channeled through life insurance, there's no need to constantly monitor it. Policies are stable because they are defined by a contract, and they are not dependent upon the ebbs and flows of the market. If there's a safer way to position your money, I've not seen it.

3. Can the RATE OF RETURN be calculated? YES.

Typical wealth management revolves around accumulating assets with the hope of building a retirement nest egg and an estate to pass on. Stocks, bonds, real estate, and mutual funds always vary. Your rate of return is unknowable and constantly changing. This is known as **"paper wealth."**

However, when you build your wealth around properly structured whole life insurance, there is a specific death benefit in place. If that number is $2 million, for example, you now own that number. It's not a hope or a wish. That is what you will be passing on to your heirs. This is known as **"contract wealth"** because the insurance company is obligated to pay when you die. You know your rate of return. You pay a defined sum into the contract, and you get a $2 million payment. Contractually, your death benefit will always be greater than your deposits.

4. Are there any TAX BENEFITS? YES.

The government is set up to tax assets, revenue, and profits. But life insurance benefits are considered tax-exempt. They have to be because they don't fall into those categories. A contract is considered a contract where a company agrees to pay you a certain amount of money when you die. The reason it's not taxed is because it is the replacement of an asset or your Human Life Value.

5. Is there an EXIT STRATEGY? YES.

With life insurance, you have the ultimate exit strategy. But you can actually pull money out at any time by borrowing against the contract. And you can reload it at any time, as well. Your opportunity fund lets you exit any time you want, for whatever reason you have, whether for business or personal reasons, while preserving your family and estate. (For more information, read *Live Your Life Insurance* by Kim Butler. I highly recommend it.)

WHERE DO BANKS PUT THEIR MONEY?

I hope your mind is opening up and you're beginning to see the advantages of life insurance beyond the death benefit. And if you need more convincing, consider this: Do you want to put your money with the banks or where the banks put their money? A bank purchases what's known as Bank Owned Life Insurance (BOLI) with either a single premium or a series of annual premiums on a select group of key employees and/or bank directors. The bank is the owner and the beneficiary, although many banks opt to share a portion of the insurance proceeds with the participants. The tax-adjusted cash value growth within the BOLI contract produces a return greater than the opportunity cost of what the bank would have made in an alternative investment if it had not purchased BOLI.

BOLI is a tax-favored asset with returns that typically exceed after-tax returns of more typical bank investments, such as municipal bond funds, mortgage-backed securities, and 5-year and 10-year Treasuries by 150 to 300 basis points.

Look at how much life insurance the banks own:

BANKS RANKED BY LIFE INSURANCE ASSETS

The following is a ranking of the top 20 banks in the United States in terms of "Life Insurance Assets." This comparison is based on data reported on 03/31/2024.

RANK	LIFE INSURANCE ASSETS	BANK NAME
1	$24,221,000,000	Bank of America
2	$18,339,000,000	Wells Fargo Bank
3	$12,465,000,000	JPMorgan Chase Bank
4	$11,212,632,000	PNC Bank
5	$7,690,000,000	Truist Bank
6	$7,671,594,000	U.S. Bank
7	$5,317,000,000	Citibank
8	$4,676,000,000	The Bank of New York Mellon
9	$4,440,979,000	BMO Bank
10	$4,193,815,000	KeyBank
11	$3,770,000,000	State Street Bank and Trust Company
12	$3,475,000,000	Regions Bank
13	$3,264,336,000	Citizens Bank
14	$2,710,539,000	The Huntington National Bank
15	$2,259,573,000	The Northern Trust Company
16	$2,108,000,000	Fifth Third Bank
17	$1,978,484,000	Capital One
18	$1,976,180,000	Santander Bank, N.A.
19	$1,808,966,000	TD Bank
20	$1,586,000,000	Flagstar Bank

https://www.usbanklocations.com/bank-rank/life-insurance-assets.html

So, if we know the primary focus of banks is on making a profit and they dedicate and deposit this much money into life insurance, they must know that life insurance is a good thing.

When you pursue true wealth, it's critical to know and understand the facts and benefits of life insurance. Put aside the misconceptions you've always believed about life insurance and explore the real opportunity it gives you.

Peak Performance Tip #14

Maybe we should do **WHAT** the banks do
and **NOT** what they tell us to do.

FIFTEEN

THE TAX-FREE MONEY BOX

A MAN WHO DIES WITHOUT ADEQUATE LIFE INSURANCE SHOULD HAVE TO COME BACK AND SEE THE MESS HE CREATED.

—WILL ROGERS

Isn't technology amazing? With a modern-day cell phone, we hold in our hands the ability to take pictures, navigate directions, surf the web, shop for concert tickets, listen to books and music, check the weather, watch movies, pay bills, play games, and so much more! The list goes on and on. Incidentally, you can also use a cell phone to make phone calls (boring!).

Permanent life insurance is similar in a lot of ways. Yes, there is a death benefit, and that's important. But that's just the tip of the iceberg.

Recently, in Newport Beach, CA, I was riding in a new Mercedes with a very prominent wealth advisor.

"How did you finance this car?" I asked him.

He answered, "Oh, I just paid cash for it." I wasn't too surprised since he has more money than he knows what to do with, but I was surprised that he didn't know how our Wealth in Overdrive® strategy could have saved him thousands of dollars over his lifetime in unnecessary costs.

I mentioned to him that Americans today finance everything we buy. I shared that there are typically three ways to finance his car, and they all have costs attached to them:

❶ Pay cash.

❷ Borrow the money from a lending institution.

❸ Lease it from the manufacturer.

I spent the next three minutes explaining how there is a better, more efficient strategy with tax advantages attached to it—the Wealth in Overdrive® strategy. I told him how on my last car purchase, I borrowed the money against my life insurance policy and paid cash for the car. I then leased the car through my corporation, and I asked him, "Guess where the lease payments go?" He had no idea. So I told him, "Back to reload my life insurance policy while tax-deducting the lease payments to my corporation and still earning interest and dividends on money I borrowed against my contract."

Needless to say, he was blown away. The surprised look on his face said it all: "That's quite brilliant!" he said. He's now one of my clients. And that's the power of applying an uncommon solution to a common problem.

As I explained in the previous chapter, a life insurance contract can become a flexible, risk-free, tax-free, flow-through entity for accumulating assets. It can provide every opportunity you need to invest in stocks, bonds, real estate, and all the other vehicles used by typical financial advisors. And, rather than having to lock your money away, you have the opportunity to USE your assets while you actually live out your dreams during the years before the death benefit ever comes into play.

The time has come for us to stop figuratively treating our cell phones like landlines, and that all begins with understanding what we actually hold in our hands. Allow me to expound on just a few of the many opportunities that are at your disposal with a properly designed life insurance contract.

15 (OF 70) BENEFITS OF THE TAX-FREE MONEY BOX
(SEE APPENDIX TWO)

BENEFIT #1: Family Provision

We may as well begin with the death benefit. If you think about it, life insurance is the only type of coverage where the event is guaranteed to happen. Almost everyone has car, health, and homeowners insurance, yet not everyone will have a car accident, surgery, or a house fire. Other than peace of mind, we spend a whole lot of money on insurance without reaping any benefits. Life insurance is the exception.

Death is the only thing in life that's 100% certain (besides paying taxes). One way or another, it will eventually payout, which means it's one of the best ways to provide maximum protection for your family. We need to be able to match a guaranteed event with a guaranteed contract that allows you to live the life you want. Remember, you own that number of the death benefit the day you sign the contract.

I'll never forget one of my clients from a few years ago. After one of my workshops, she approached me, saying she was ready to move forward with me as her wealth advisor. She said she was ready to make life insurance the foundation of her plan.

Together, we spent multiple hours putting together a beautiful, well-laid-out, comprehensive plan that included wills, trusts, an investment portfolio, and a life insurance contract specifically designed, coordinated, and integrated with her business. I printed out all the pages, and the only thing missing was her signature. Despite my urging, she chose to wait until she returned from a well-deserved two-week vacation in Hawaii to finalize it. I decided to email the life insurance contract to her so she could read and e-sign it while she was on her trip. Unfortunately, she suffered a stroke during her time away and was unable to sign. Although she was in her early fifties and in very good health, she slipped into a coma and never woke up. That unsigned will and trust and the unsigned life insurance contract still haunts me to this day.

What a regrettable situation that was. Her family will never have access to that money because of one missing mouse click. Can you also imagine the nightmare her heirs went through settling her estate?

Unfortunately, I have all too many stories like this. There was the Ford executive who, at age fifty-eight, told me he didn't believe in permanent life insurance and planned on canceling his $2 million term contract at age sixty-five. He'd taken good care of his body, but he had an antiquated mindset about life insurance. He ended up dying at sixty-seven while working out in the gym. His refusal to entertain the idea of life insurance cost his family $2 million tax-free. And because his term life insurance contract expired when he turned sixty-five, his family completely missed out. He thought he only **needed** the coverage to age sixty-five.

People often ask me, "How much coverage should I have?" As a general rule of thumb, I suggest that people are entitled to one million dollars of coverage for every $50,000 income they earn or one times their net worth, whichever is greater.

I even knew of a couple under the age of forty with two small kids who ran a business that had been averaging about $360,000 a year in revenue. While on vacation in Las Vegas, the husband choked to death on a piece of food. I was shocked and frustrated to find out that his life insurance contract was only worth $500,000. It made me want to hunt down his insurance agent and sue him for malpractice. For a healthy thirty-nine-year-old male with so much at stake, a $500,000 contract wasn't nearly enough protection. For a mere $2,500 more per year, he could have had a $6,000,000 term insurance contract. And it would have been worth every penny. Financially, I consider it a travesty. Now his widowed wife is struggling to keep the business afloat, and the family isn't sure what the future holds.

Like it or not, life insurance is one of the surest ways to create an estate and provide for your family.

BENEFIT #2: Disability Protection

No one wants to experience a disability. Some people refer to it as "the living death" because the bills continue to show up every month despite the fact that you are incapacitated and unable to work. What many people are unaware of is that life insurance often comes with what is referred to as the "disability premium waiver." A disability premium waiver is a clause that states that if the insured person were to become disabled and unable to make his premium payments, the insurance company would cover that cost. Perhaps it should be called "the premium continuation" instead, as it allows the contract's cash value to keep building even in the event of a disability.

No other financial product has this feature. Certainly, your stockbroker wouldn't continue to deposit money into your investment portfolio if you became disabled. Your employer wouldn't continue dumping money into your 401(k) if you were disabled. No other financial product will continue your financial plan in the event of a disability. In fact, even a disability insurance contract can't do this because it's only designed to provide a portion of a person's income to cover basic living needs.

BENEFIT #3: Asset Protection

Let's face it. We live in an age of lawsuits. They happen all the time, and they can potentially destroy the financial lives of families and businesses. So, it is wise to secure some sort of asset protection against possible litigation, even if you think it will never happen to you.

Life insurance provides protection against lawsuits involving your home, qualified retirement plans, irrevocable trust assets, and permanent life insurance cash values (in most states). A permanent life insurance contract itself is also protected from lawsuits and creditors in most states, which means that lenders can't force the owner of a contract to drop the coverage to meet any sort of debt obligation.

Another unique feature of life insurance is that the cash values of the policies aren't disclosed on college financial aid forms (FAFSA).

By allowing parents to keep cash values unrevealed, college-bound dependents may qualify for additional grants, scholarships, or work-study programs. Conversely, 529 plan balances DO have to be disclosed and may work against you.

BENEFIT #4: Private Non-Recourse Personal Loans

America is a nation of consumers. In an article published by a magazine called *Fast Company*, Polly LaBarre states, "The United States spends more on trash bags than 90 other countries spend on everything. In other words, the receptacles of our waste cost more than all of the goods consumed by nearly half of the world's nations."[21]

For good or bad, we live in a country where people like to buy "stuff." The beauty of life insurance is that you are free to borrow against your contract and spend the money on whatever you desire, whether for consumption or investment purposes. And you can do this without worrying about collateral, outrageous interest rates, credit scores, or lengthy loan papers.

The cash value and death benefit of the contract act as collateral for your loan. And because you've provided that collateral, your loan comes with a much lower interest rate. And there's no need to worry about your credit score because you have fully collateralized the loan.

Also, personal loans against your contract do not affect the growth potential of the cash value of your contract. That is to say, **you aren't stopping the uninterrupted compounded, tax-free growth of your exponential curve**. Remember, you're borrowing against it, not from it. This is such an **IMPORTANT POINT** that I really want to make sure you grasp the magnitude of it all.

Imagine depositing $10,000 into a CD that would earn 5%. If you were able to withdraw $3,000 the next day for a temporary loan, it would be your balance of $7,000 that would now be earning 5%. But if you did the same thing with your life insurance contract, you'd continue to earn dividends and interest on the full sum of $10,000, even though the account would have a net equity balance of $7,000! This is a tremendous benefit, and many people do not even know it exists.

The reason this works is because the insurer is merely advancing you money **against** the cash reserves in your contract and the death benefit. It doesn't change the value of your contract any more than a home equity line of credit would change the appraisal value of your house. More importantly, it is a non-recourse loan. **It doesn't even show up on your credit report.**

And an insurance loan obligation only comes due at death. Before then, the owner of the contract is able to set the repayment terms of the loan. He can reload his contract **when** he wants, **how** he wants, or even **if** he wants.

BENEFIT #5: Tax Benefits

In 1997, a CPA explained these tax benefits to me, and it forever changed my perspective on life insurance.

When you borrow against your life insurance, it stays off the radar screen of the IRS. That's because you are borrowing against your own asset. This is a huge financial advantage. According to page 27 of the **1990 GAO (General Accounting Office) Report**, the Tax Policy **"Tax Treatment of Life Insurance,"** states, "<u>If a contract holder borrows the inside buildup from his or her life insurance contract, the amount borrowed is considered a transfer of capital, not a real-</u>

ization of income, and, therefore, is not subject to taxation. This reasoning is in accord with tax policy on other types of loans, such as consumer loans or home mortgages. These loans are merely transfers of capital or savings from one person to another through a financial intermediary."[22]

The report goes on to say, "The ability to borrow against a life insurance contract means that the interest income that is supposed to be building up to fund death benefits can instead be a source of untaxed income. If the loans are not repaid, the inside buildup will never be taxed; death benefits will simply be reduced by the amount of the loan. Thus, policyholders have the use of tax-free income for purposes other than insurance at the expense of reduced death benefits for their beneficiaries."[23]

United States General Accounting Office

GAO

Report to the Chairman, Committee on
Finance, U.S. Senate, and the Chairman,
Committee on Ways and Means, House
of Representatives

January 1990

TAX POLICY

Tax Treatment of Life Insurance and Annuity Accrued Interest

Chapter 3
Favorable Tax Treatment of Inside Buildup
Encourages Investment-Oriented Products

Borrowing Against Inside Buildup Is Tax-Free for Life Insurance

If a policyholder borrows the inside buildup from his or her life insurance policy, the amount borrowed is considered a transfer or capital, not a realization of income, and, therefore, is not subject to taxation. This reasoning is in accord with tax policy on other types of loans, such as consumer loans or home mortgages. These loans are merely transfers or capital or savings from one person to another through a financial intermediary. The ability to borrow against a life insurance policy means that the interest income that is supposed to be building up to fund death benefits can instead be a source of untaxed current income. If the loans are not repaid, the inside buildup will never be taxed; death benefits will simply be reduced by the amount of the loan. Thus, policyholders have the use of tax-free income for purposes other than insurance at the expense of reduced death benefits for their beneficiaries.[5]

There are six IRS tax-free code provisions favoring permanent life insurance as shown in the table below:

IRS TAX CODE PROVISIONS FOR PERMANENT LIFE INSURANCE	
INCOME TAX-FREE DEATH BENEFIT IRC SECTION 101(A)(1)	**TAX-FREE WITHDRAWALS TO BASIS** IRC SECTION 72(E)
TAX-FREE BUILDUP WITHIN POLICY IRC SECTION 7702(A) AND 7702(G)	**INVESTMENT GAINS CAN BE BORROWED AGAINST POLICY WITHOUT TAXATION** IRC SECTION 72(E)(5)
ESTATE TAX-FREE DEATH BENEFIT IRC SECTION 2035	**MEC TAX-FREE BUILDUP AND DEATH BENEFIT** IRC SECTION 7702(A)

Many wise contract holders will leverage the current tax code to their benefit during their retirement years as a means of tapping into a tax-exempt income stream. Let's just say that it certainly beats withdrawing from a government-sponsored retirement plan!

BENEFIT #6: Peace of Mind

We live in a world with lots of uncertainty and instability. There's the threat of recession, depression, inflation, political unrest, stock market violence and volatility, business failures, geo-political concerns, corporate downsizing and mergers, pandemic repercussions, and more. Is it even possible to invest successfully with such unpredictable circumstances unfolding daily? Remember, your financial structure must be anchored on a firm foundation.

During the Great Depression, hundreds of banks went under. Every single mutual life insurance company, however, survived. Many even paid a dividend. If peace of mind is a financial priority, there is no better option.

The amazing thing about life insurance is that no one, I repeat, no one, has ever lost a dollar of their guaranteed funds with a legal reserve life insurance company as a result of bankruptcy.

BENEFIT #7: A Buffer against Market Volatility

Let's pretend you had a million dollars in your portfolio, and you knew in advance that you would get a 14.84% **average** rate of return over the next 30 years. Your intention is to withdraw 10% ($100,000) every year.

Straightforward math would indicate that not only would this be possible, but you'd have about $15 million remaining in your portfolio after year 30. That's not a bad deal. Take a look:

RETIREMENT YEAR	ANNUAL RETURN	ANNUAL INCOME	ACCOUNT VALUE
1	14.84%	-$100,000	$1,033,560
2	14.84%	-$100,000	$1,072,100
3	14.84%	-$100,000	$1,116,360
4	14.84%	-$100,000	$1,167,188
5	14.84%	-$100,000	$1,225,558
6	14.84%	-$100,000	$1,292,591
7	14.84%	-$100,000	$1,369,572
8	14.84%	-$100,000	$1,457,976
9	14.84%	-$100,000	$1,559,500
10	14.84%	-$100,000	$1,676,090
15	14.84%	-$100,000	$2,575,983
20	14.84%	-$100,000	$4,373,434
25	14.84%	-$100,000	$7,963,668
30	14.84%	-$100,000	$15,134,818

There's only one problem—that's not how the market resets or how money works. I repeat: **Money is not math, and math is not money.** Let's check out the history of the actual S&P 500 Index for a 30-year period (1970–1999) and get a realistic look at the market in action.

S&P 500 INDEX FOR 30-YEAR PERIOD (1970–1999)

YEAR	ANNUAL RETURN	YEAR	ANNUAL RETURN
1970	3.99%	1985	31.65%
1971	14.33%	1986	18.60%
1972	18.94%	1987	5.17%
1973	-14.79%	1988	16.61%
1974	-26.54%	1989	31.69%
1975	37.25%	1990	-3.10%
1976	23.67%	1991	30.47%
1977	-7.39%	1992	7.62%
1978	6.44%	1993	10.08%
1979	18.35%	1994	1.32%
1980	32.27%	1995	37.58%
1981	-5.05%	1996	22.96%
1982	21.48%	1997	33.36%
1983	22.50%	1998	28.58%
1984	6.15%	1999	21.04%

Despite a few negative numbers, the **average** yield for the 30-year period is still 14.84%. However, if you withdraw $100,000 a year in real time, your portfolio would run dry in year 14 because of the **Sequence of Return Risk.**

Sequence of Return Risk is what happens when the market declines in the early years of retirement while continuous withdrawals remain in place, significantly reducing the longevity of your portfolio. In other words, you run out of money.

SEQUENCE OF RETURN RISK

RETIREMENT YEAR	ANNUAL YIELD	ANNUAL INCOME	ACCOUNT VALUE
1	3.99%	-$100,000	$935,910
2	14.33%	-$100,000	$955,695
3	18.94%	-$100,000	$1,017,765
4	-14.79%	-$100,000	$782,028
5	-26.54%	-$100,000	$501,018
6	37.25%	-$100,000	$550,397
7	23.67%	-$100,000	$557,006
8	-7.39%	-$100,000	$423,233
9	6.44%	-$100,000	$344,049
10	18.35%	-$100,000	$288,832
11	32.27%	-$100,000	$249,768
12	-5.05%	-$100,000	$142,205
13	21.48%	-$100,000	$53,803
14	22.50%	-$100,000	($56,591) ← Out of money!
15	6.15%	-$100,000	($166,221)

As you can see, instead of having a nice $15 million in your account at the end of year thirty, you're now broke after only fourteen years. The **Sequence of Return Risk** (the downturn in the market) completely destroyed your plan.

The possibility of stock prices falling or bond assets declining during the early years of retirement poses perhaps the greatest risk that retirees face. This type of market volatility can completely devastate your long-term plans.

Most people don't have a solid method for insulating their accounts from the unpredictable violence of the market. The typical defense is to try to maintain a diversified portfolio and rebalance it regularly.

However, for those with permanent life insurance, there's a much better solution, endorsed by Dr. Wade Pfau, which he terms a "Volatility Buffer."[24]

> **"Using your cash reserve as a non-correlated asset to the market and as an alternate source of income during the market's down years allows you to manage your retirement income more effectively without depleting your reserve, giving your market position a chance to recover."**
>
> —Dr. Wade Pfau

Scan this QR code to read Dr. Pfau's and Michael Finke's article, "Integrating Whole Life Insurance into a Retirement Income Plan."

If there's one thing we learned from the 2008 financial crisis and recession that followed, it was the importance of having another source of income that's **not correlated to the market** during a prolonged downtime. In other words, when times are tough, eating the goose who is laying the golden eggs shouldn't be your only option. Make no mistake: **the volatility buffer strategy advantage of using life insurance provides you with the greatest protection against outliving your assets.**

"Our analysis showed Permanent Life Insurance integrated with investment strategies outperform investment-only and term life + investment strategies.

Integrated strategies provide investors with the flexibility to focus on the financial outcomes most important to them; retirement income, legacy or a balance in between."[25]

—Ernst & Young, LLP

Scan this QR code to read "How Life Insurers Can Provide Differentiated Retirement Benefits," by Justin Singer of Ernst & Young.

BENEFIT #8: Taxes and Inflation Protection

Imagine a world without taxes and inflation. I know that seems laughable, if not impossible. They're both cornerstones of the American market. However, we can use some of the unique properties of a permanent life insurance plan to offset the erosion caused by both taxes and inflation.

Properly designed life insurance allows us to utilize our homes, savings, and investments in new and creative ways to counteract the impact of taxes and inflation. Many retirees fear they will spend down their savings and simply run out of money. Leveraging your plan correctly will alleviate these headaches and worries.

BENEFIT #9: Leverage the Death Benefit

The typical American tends to think too linearly when it comes to retirement. There is a smarter way to employ your money than to simply stockpile it and live off the interest with the hope that your money will outlast your life.

The death benefit of a permanent life insurance contract gives you the opportunity to **spend and enjoy your wealth without the fear of running out**. You can leverage it against illnesses, long-term care, creditors, and taxes. It's like walking around with a winning lottery ticket in your pocket that your heirs can cash in when you die. But remarkably, you don't have to die to capitalize on the benefits! It's your permission slip to enjoy your money while you are still alive.

When you transition from your working life to retirement life, the purpose of your life insurance transitions as well. **It makes the change from income protection to asset protection.**

BENEFIT #10: Turbocharge of Assets

In 1968, race car driver Bobby Unser won the Indy 500 by driving a car equipped with a turbocharger. This one key move substantially revolutionized the future of race car driving. The turbocharger provided an extraordinary boost to his vehicle through better fuel efficiency.

Permanent life insurance can be used in a similar way. When used correctly, it can provide a massive spark to your other financial assets resulting in a much better, more efficient financial outcome.

Many people confuse life insurance as an investment option. "Should I purchase a contract **OR** invest in real estate?" They are looking at it the wrong way. It's not an either/or decision. It's an **"AND"** decision. Life insurance, real estate, and investments work together to produce a better outcome. In other words, **life insurance is the turbocharger, not the engine.** By redirecting cash flow, interest, dividends, capital gains, investments, and savings through the "turbocharger," you can achieve much better results. Walt Disney, Ray Kroc, J. C. Penney, and Doris Christopher didn't get rich off their policies. They used their policies to acquire and expand their businesses and wealth.

> **REMEMBER, LIFE INSURANCE IS A BETTER DISTRIBUTION VEHICLE, NOT AN ACCUMULATION VEHICLE. IT HAS THE ABILITY TO AMPLIFY ALL YOUR OTHER ASSETS. IT'S LIKE ADDING SALT TO YOUR FOOD.**

BENEFIT #11: Liquidity

Believe it or not, depending on the design of the life insurance contract, most people can request funds from their plan within a week of purchasing it. It's as simple as making a phone call.

Some companies may require the completion of a cash surrender or loan request form, but that's it. It's not like filling out a loan application at a bank and waiting for approval. You have access to your money in no time. It doesn't get any more liquid than that. No wonder it's listed as a liquid asset on bank financial statements.

BENEFIT #12: Reverse Mortgage

Did you know that you can make money off your house while you're still living in it? How is this possible?

It's possible through reverse mortgages, most of which are available to individuals over sixty-two.

In a reverse mortgage, a financial institution will pay you either a lump sum of money or a monthly income based on your age and the equity in the residence. They pay you principal only, which is key because it means you pay no income tax, and the payments aren't included in the determination of tax on your Social Security. You are charged interest, but it's not due until either the death of the contract owner or the sale of the property. The bank can't demand payment while you're living, so there's no fear of losing your house during your lifetime.

Many people eligible for these types of home equity conversion mortgages (HECM) are afraid of them. They worry that, when their spouse dies, they may not have enough money to pay off the debt on the house, especially if they have to sell in a hurry. Having a life insurance plan in place serves as a backup to pay a reverse mortgage obligation, thus eliminating the fear of winding up broke and homeless. The death benefit is the key that unlocks your home, like a pension.

BENEFIT #13: Private Asset

Because a life insurance contract is defined as "a legal unilateral contract between the owner of the contract and the issuing insurance company," it's considered a private transaction. This means that you, the contract holder, are not always required to disclose the contract on any sort of financial form that might come your way. Thus, you have protection against any lawsuit or creditors (in most states).

In fact, upon your death, if set up properly, the contract will pass to a named beneficiary and bypass probate court and all the publicity and headaches associated with this process. This is a huge benefit!

BENEFIT #14: Optimal Estate Planning

When we die, we have five potential beneficiaries: family, charity, estate sale purchasers, financial institutions, or the IRS. Of those five, where do you want to leave your estate?

Most people would much rather have their estate end up with family or charity instead of strangers, banks, or the IRS. Most people would also love to have a low-cost estate plan that allows them to enjoy their wealth while they are still living.

Unfortunately, if wishes were fishes, we'd all swim in riches. It's so much easier said than done.

Estate planning can be complicated and costly in both time and money. Many people lock up their assets in sophisticated irrevocable trusts, which, for the most part, can't be touched during their lifetime.

THE BEST ESTATE PLANS SHOULD INCLUDE THESE THREE MAIN OBJECTIVES:

❶ Getting **WHAT** you have, to **WHO** you want it to go to, **WHEN** you want it to go to them, under **YOUR** chosen terms and conditions. **Control from beyond the grave.**

❷ Eradicate the exposure to **DIVORCE, LAWSUIT,** and **TRANSFER TAXES** on your wealth **FOREVER.**

❸ Provide you with the satisfactory multiple streams of **INCOME** and **CONTROL.**

"A LEGACY IS A SEED YOU PLANT. YOU DON'T ALWAYS GET TO SEE THE FRUIT DURING YOUR LIFETIME."

—PHIL BODINE

Now, as great as life insurance is and as free as it can be of income taxes, it's not necessarily free of taxes for those wishing to designate their estate as the beneficiary. That's why many people are told to have an irrevocable life insurance trust on their contract. Unfortunately, that locks up the cash value from being used for many of the wealth strategies we've discussed.

The question that has to be asked is whether it's worth losing the additional creation of wealth or the enjoyment of wealth that can come from owning it outside of the trust. And the answer should be a resounding "No!" Imagine how foolish it would seem to place your home into an irrevocable trust, where you couldn't live in it, enjoy it, sell it, or use any of the equity, all for the sake of saving estate tax. Yet, that's exactly what many well-meaning attorneys, estate planners, and accountants recommend with life insurance.

If the estate tax were eliminated, the life insurance contract owned by an irrevocable life insurance trust would be hard to undo and very costly to unravel. A better alternative might be to secure the maximum amount of permanent life insurance coverage that a company will issue you while you are healthy. This would allow you to enjoy life to the fullest by using all of your assets during your lifetime.

This is a strategy that will give you more freedom, more flexibility, and more control. You are the one in charge of all financial decisions, not the bank or your heirs.

**ALERT! FINANCIAL AWARENESS!
DON'T MAKE "THE MULTI-MILLION DOLLAR MISTAKE"!**

Think of it this way: If I work from age 25 to 65, make $100,000 per year of income, and pay $25,000 in taxes every year for 40 years, then I will take $1,000,000 away from my family as a loss due to federal income taxes. **THE COSTS DON'T STOP THERE. THE LOST OPPORTUNITY COST OF THE TAX PAID IS ONGOING!** If I live another 30 years of my life until age 95, then the $1,000,000 lost in taxes paid is compounding to a larger loss to my family.

Calculation: $1,000,000 present value at 6% lost opportunity costs (LOC) compounded annually would equal $5,743,491 in future value over a 30-year period.

If I do nothing to recapture the $1,000,000 of taxes paid and the $5,743,491 in LOC at my death, then this will continue to compound to my grandkids at the death of my youngest child 40 years after I am gone—that LOC being equal to $59,075,930 ($5,743,491 @ 6% LOC for 40 years).

These dollars of wealth were lost because I did not have a financial strategy to recapture the taxes paid and LOC over my lifetime. Life insurance can provide this solution. Everyone can become a millionaire who plans for certainty and leaves specific tax-free dollars properly structured for future and generational wealth, just like the wise and wealthy (Rockefeller Waterfall Method).

What do you have in place right now that will guarantee your great-grandkids can recapture the money you have paid in income taxes over your working lifetime? Have any of your other advisors ever shared that with you?

It's not about how much money you make but how much money you keep, how hard it works for you, and how many generations you keep it for.

—Robert Kiyosaki

BENEFIT #15: Internal, External, and Eternal Rate of Return

Internal Rate of Return is the earnings growth rate inside a financial product or asset.

> **Example:** A mutual fund has an average Internal Rate of Return of 8% over a 20-year period.

External Rate of Return is the net earnings growth rate after outside forces have decreased the internal rate of return.

> **Example:** A mutual fund has an 8% Internal Rate of Return, but after commissions, fees, and taxes, it has an External Rate of Return of 5%.

Eternal Rate of Return is the net earnings growth rate of a financial product or asset caused by the death of the owner.

> **Example:** A mutual fund has an external net rate of return of 5%. At the death of the account owner, it may have an Eternal Rate of Return of 2% after income taxes, estate taxes, inheritance taxes, attorney fees, and accounting fees.

Many financial advisors focus strictly on the internal buildup of investments and/or life insurance's equity values. And they only calculate that rate to be somewhere between 3% and 10% a year.

However, the external rate of return can be even more profound. External rate of return is what permanent life insurance allows you to do with assets that are normally frozen or minimized. When you employ some of the life insurance strategies like pension maximization, spend down, and reverse mortgages we've discussed, you're receiving the equivalent of an additional 10% to 15% after-tax rate of return.

And while the internal and external rate of return are important, it's the eternal rate of return that provides the ultimate benefit. It refers to the death benefit that is actually paid out to our beneficiaries.

While studies have shown that many Americans have life insurance, many own term life insurance policies, which means that the vast majority of the $12.4 trillion of life insurance in force today will never pay a death benefit. By owning a permanent life insurance plan, your eternal rate of return will have a long-term, far-reaching impact on those you care about the most. And these benefits have the potential to extend for generations to come. That's not a bad legacy to leave behind.

I've often thought that owning life insurance is, in and of itself, an act of love for family, community, charity, business, or oneself. And it's the overarching reason why purchasing life insurance is one of the most prudent financial decisions you can make. Make no mistake—the truly wealthy people of the world not only understand how to generate great riches, but they also put plans in place for distributing it to their heirs for generations to come. And properly designed life insurance is a pebble in a pond that creates a ripple effect on internal, external, and eternal rates of return.

INTERNAL, EXTERNAL, AND ETERNAL = RATE OF RESULTS

A properly structured contract set up through cash flow life insurance is the only tool that is able to successfully unite all fifteen of those components to create the ideal financial plan.

And that's . . . something to call home about.

FINANCIAL PRODUCTS AND THEIR BENEFITS

Type of Asset	Stocks/ Mutual Funds	Bonds Taxable	Muni Bonds	CD's MM's	ROTH IRA/ 401(k)	Traditional 401(k)	Real Estate	Accumulation Annuities	Whole Life Insurance
Unlimited Savings Participation	✓	✓	✓	✓			✓	✓	✓
Tax-Free Accumulation			✓		✓	✓	✓	✓	✓
Tax-Free Distribution			✓		✓				✓
Guarantee of Principal				✓					✓
Minimize Risk of Loss				✓				✓	✓
Ease of Access				✓					✓
Unlimited Access w/o Tax or Penalty									✓
Creditor Protection									✓
Disability Protection of Savings									✓
Provision for Death									✓
Provision for LTC									✓
Higher Internal Rate of Return	✓				✓	✓			

Peak Performance Tip #15

Value protection at a premium even above opportunity. The reality about **PERMANENT LIFE INSURANCE** is that it should be the **CENTERPIECE** of any **SUCCESSFUL WEALTH-BUILDING STRATEGY** with certainty.

Connect With Us!

If you would like to subscribe to the **Wealth in Overdrive**® podcast, keep up to date with future events and **Wealth in Overdrive**® workshops, or set up a one-on-one consultation with one of our registered team members, simply scan the QR code below.

SIXTEEN

FINDING THE RIGHT ADVISOR

A GOOD COACH CAN CHANGE A GAME. A GREAT COACH CAN CHANGE A LIFE.

—JOHN WOODEN

Money isn't everything. In fact, money may not be the most important thing in your world ... but it affects everything that is. It affects your lifestyle, your choices, your healthcare, and your level of education. It even affects the food you eat and your quality of life on a day-to-day basis.[26]

MONEY AFFECTS EVERYTHING

IT AFFECTS YOUR
LIFESTYLE

IT AFFECTS YOUR
HEALTHCARE

"Money may not be the most important thing in your world... But it affects everything that is."[26]

IT AFFECTS YOUR
LEVEL OF
EDUCATION

IT AFFECTS
EVERYTHING
ON A DAY-TO-DAY BASIS

IT AFFECTS THE
FOOD YOU EAT

There's no denying that money is an important part of life. And unfortunately, in our country, we don't do a very good job of educating young people on the topic. It's probably why there are so many financial advisors in business today. I mean, someone has to know how money works, right?

Even if you were educated on money and currently have a strong financial awareness, staying on top of everything takes an enormous amount of time, energy, resources, and research.

People often ask me, "How important is it to have a financial advisor? Do I really even need one at all?" Can you imagine what an orchestra would sound like if all the musicians were playing off different sheets of music with no conductor to guide them? It would definitely NOT be music to your ears.

Yet, many people have all kinds of financial advisors playing off different sheets of "financial music" with no one there to guide them. Each one of these "financial" musicians are what I call "Micro Managers." They're specialists. They know their instruments well, but rarely do they act in concert with each other. They are not coordinated or integrated to make a beautiful harmony.

To achieve real financial success, you need a **"Macro Manager"** or a conductor. He's the one who will keep all your Micro Managers on the same page so that everything flows in harmony. Let me ask you one important question. When was the last time all your advisors gathered in a room to talk about you and your plan?

"REMEMBER, **WHO** YOU WORK WITH **MATTERS**."

—PHIL BODINE

MACRO-MANAGING YOUR FINANCIAL LIFE

Having a wise financial advisor is like having a money coach who helps you instill discipline. If you have the time, knowledge, and interest, there is no reason to have a financial advisor. However, a good financial coach will help you accomplish your financial goals more quickly, with less anxiety, less taxes, and fewer mistakes. Investors who utilize a high-quality advisor often feel more confident and optimistic, and they are significantly more likely to stick to their plans versus trying to do it themselves. And though the market is full of advisors, it can be challenging to find a good one. So don't be in a hurry. Take your time and find a competent advisor or even a team of specialists. **Who you work with does matter!**

So, how does one go about finding a really good advisor? How do you discern the good from the bad? It's not easy. It's like trying to tell the difference between a good lawyer and a bad lawyer when you've never used one. The same could be said for plumbers, accountants, architects, or any type of professional. While it may seem logical to simply follow recommendations made by family and friends, you should remember that with money, not all philosophies are the same. And not all advisors have your best interests at heart. A good advisor tells you what you **need** to hear, not exactly what you **want** to hear.

Many people assume that most large wirehouse firms must have a full array of top-notch products and services with the best-trained advisors in the industry. Certainly, they must know what they are doing, right? Their ads are everywhere! Plus, they "promise" to meet all our financial needs.

Unfortunately, most investment firms operate in a way that works best for them, not necessarily for you. They want you to park your assets in the same place for a really long time. And when retirement does come, they want you to withdraw as little as possible. The longer you stretch it out, the longer they remain in control of your money. Sound familiar? And somehow, everyone thinks this is a great idea. It's ludicrous! Who wants to work hard for forty years and then live off as little as possible during the Golden Years?

Big firms also love to spotlight investment portfolios. They become laser-focused on what they like to call "assets under management" (AUM). An associate of mine has strong ties to friends at well-known wirehouse firms. He once asked one of their top advisors about their holistic philosophies. In other words, how much does the company train its advisors to delve into areas like disability, asset protection, tax planning, estate planning, or life insurance? The advisor's response: "Not much." Again, big firms typically focus on investment portfolio products and don't normally target areas involving life insurance because:

1. It takes too much time.

Big-named firms are all about efficiency and scale. They want to automate trading and generate investment advice on a company-wide basis. Insurance would be viewed as a complicated distraction requiring more training for their advisors. It's too much work, and it's not necessary for the success of their bottom line.

2. There's not enough money.

Advisors wouldn't make enough money on the fees from insurance to warrant taking their attention off the coveted investment portfolio.

3. They have inferior insurance products.

Most big companies can't offer the best insurance products because they don't own any. They own investment products. In-house products always have the largest profit margins. So that's what they focus on. Unless they have an insurance product of their own, odds are investment firms aren't going to steer clients in that direction. Why send revenue to an outside source like a mutual contract holder when their primary focus is to benefit the shareholder?!

Even many smaller firms and solo practitioners fall into the same trap of ignoring key planning details by focusing primarily on investment portfolios where the ultimate goal, again, is to accumulate AUM. As I mentioned earlier, I subscribed to this blueprint for the first two and a half years of my career. I was just trying to survive, so I followed the industry protocol. But eventually, I began challenging the system and seeking mentors who knew better. And it opened my eyes. In my early days, I didn't even want to touch insurance. Now, every comprehensive financial plan I put together revolves around it.

I mentioned this quote before by highly respected author Dr. Wade Pfau, a professor of retirement planning at the American College of Financial Services, and it's worth repeating:

> **"The financial services profession is generally divided between two camps: those focusing on investment solutions and those focusing on insurance solutions. My research shows that the most efficient retirement strategies require an integration of both investments and insurance."**[27]

So many financial planners in the industry just follow the book, not realizing that the book is outdated. Typical strategies promoted by financial institutions are designed to help the institution first, not the client. Remember, **Wall Street promotes risk**. In fact, Wall Street has a favorite formula. It goes like this:

$$W = M \times R \times T$$

That is to say, Wealth = Money x Rate x Time. It sounds great, but the truth is, it simply doesn't work. It's a massively flawed formula. Why?

✻ It won't work if you don't put enough Money into the plan.

* It won't work if you're not willing to take enough **Risk**.

* It won't work if you don't have enough **Time**.

* Plus, **Wealth = M x R x T** doesn't take into account the economic eroding factors of a more comprehensive approach.

Real wealth is generated from getting multiple rates of return on your money, not just one. With Wall Street, you're the one at risk, not the advisor, and certainly not the firm.

It's more efficient to simply steer a client toward a much-hyped 15-year mortgage than it is to explain why a 30-year mortgage is the wiser choice. Who has the time to explain why a 401(k) is the riskiest place to put your money, especially when your company is willing to match your investment?

I had a friend who once worked for one of the more well-known "prestigious" companies. He got his hand slapped for taking on an elderly lady client with limited assets, as her account would not generate any revenue for the firm. Regardless, my friend continued to assist her. Eight months later, she walked back into his office and informed my friend that she had just won the lottery, telling him, "You were the only one who took the time to assist me when I needed help. Will you please take this check and manage it for me?" She then handed him a check for $6 million. That's the kind of advisor you want.

The definition of a client is someone who comes under the umbrella and the protection of someone else. In the case of finances, the protector would be your financial advisor, whose **FIDUCIARY DUTY** is to look after your best interests. I recommend looking for

someone who subscribes to that philosophy and is not only an inde-
pendent advisor but also has the following:

* a customer-first philosophy

* a solid reputation

* quick to listen

* good communication skills

* a clear strategy

* a comprehensive macro approach including all
  advisors

* a developed and refined planning process

* a good support team

* flexibility

* lots of patience

You may have to pay more for personalized service, but it will
be worth it in the long run. I was always taught not to be penny-
wise and dollar-foolish. Or, as Red Adair stated, **"If you think it's
expensive to hire a professional, wait until you hire an amateur."**[28]

As a general rule, I recommend avoiding product-based planners. It's better to pursue strategy-based advisors. You'll net better
results in the end.

For example, if you were learning to play golf, what's more
important for your overall game?

"IF YOU THINK IT'S EXPENSIVE TO **HIRE A PROFESSIONAL**, WAIT UNTIL YOU HIRE AN AMATEUR."

– RED ADAIR

WHICH IS MORE IMPORTANT?

PRODUCTS	VS	STRATEGY

EQUIPMENT AND TOOLS   SKILL AND TECHNIQUE

Option A: A pro shop sales associate who sells you the most expensive clubs?

Option B: A golf pro who teaches you how to swing a club and navigate your way around the golf course?

In other words, would you rather have good clubs or a good swing? I have an antique golf club in my office that must be eighty years old. It has a wooden shaft and is well past its prime. Yet, I am confident that if Phil Mickelson were to use it, he could still beat any of us armed with modern-day clubs. Strategy, technique, and execution will almost always beat the product.

I had a new client walk into my office once carrying all his financial statements from his previous advisor. I was horrified. This business owner was being charged a $1,500-a-year financial planning fee. Looking over his paperwork, I immediately spotted over a dozen red flags in his current plan that had been overlooked. There was no strategy or attention to detail, and the more we conversed, the more I realized that his former advisor was the one calling all the shots. There was no rhyme or reason and certainly no explanation or understanding. This client never learned how to approach his finances. In other words, he never learned how to swing his club or felt any ownership of his plan.

Wall Street will tell you that the club is more important than the swing. I hope you realize that the effectiveness of the club is a byproduct of the perfected swing and not the other way around. Remember that Wall Street is the one manufacturing the clubs and has a vested interest in getting you to keep buying the next shiny new gimmick. Do not let the tail wag the dog when it comes to your money.

When I consider the people I admire most in the financial world, I realize they all have a few things in common:

* They care about their clients and work hard to personalize each plan to meet each individual's specific wants and dreams.

* They ask good questions, listen intently to the answers, see the big picture, and lead with a strategy.

* They practice humility.

These are hard qualities to find in anyone. And yet, they make up the common characteristics of all good financial advisors.

I occasionally think back to my dad's first experience with a financial advisor. The person he worked with was pretty good in the grand scheme of things. He wasn't overly comprehensive, but he did care a lot about our family. I'm quite certain he didn't maximize my parents' financial potential, but he did develop a good relationship with us. And that counted for a lot in the long run.

My father passed away when I was a junior in college. However, my mom stayed in pretty good shape for quite some time. She finally ran out of retirement money at age ninety-one. At that point, my four brothers and I stepped in and took care of her until she died at age ninety-three.

Your financial health is a huge cornerstone that impacts practically every aspect of your life, as well as your family, in some form or another. With that in mind, it's vital to find a person you can trust who has your best interests in mind. Don't short-change finding a good advisor just to get the ball rolling.

Exercise due diligence. And remember, before you invest your money, take your time. Find the advisor who's right for you.

Peak Performance Tip #16

Who you work with matters!

Find a **FINANCIAL ADVISOR**
who believes it is their **FIDUCIARY DUTY**
to look after **YOUR BEST INTERESTS**.

"IF THERE IS NO HOPE IN **YOUR FUTURE**, THERE IS NO POWER IN **YOUR PRESENT**."

—JOHN C. MAXWELL

SEVENTEEN

FOUR STEPS TO PLANNING YOUR RETIREMENT

THE GOAL ISN'T MORE MONEY, THE GOAL IS LIVING LIFE ON YOUR TERMS.

—WILL ROGERS

You spend your working life turning income into assets; you spend your retirement turning assets into income. Have you ever taken the time to talk to someone who can help you do that in the optimal and most tax-efficient way possible?

Many people don't know where to begin when it comes to planning for retirement. It's such a vast topic with so many variables. However, with regard to finances, you're in luck. I'm going to make it easy for you by outlining four basic steps.

STEP ONE:
DEFINE WHAT RETIREMENT MEANS TO YOU

What comes to mind when you think of retirement? Often, we think of things like lying around in a hammock all morning sipping lemonade, playing golf all afternoon, spending time with the grand-kids, or taking trips around the world.

For me, my personal definition of retirement has always been: "Having the ability to do what I want to do when I want to do it." I want to be able to work two or three days a week and spend the rest of my time with the people I love the most, doing the things I love to do. That's what retirement looks like for me.

So, what does it look like for you? The clearer you can define that picture, the easier it will be to begin formulating a plan to help you reach that dream.

Many people merely have a vague idea in their mind. They say things like, "I just want to have enough money to survive." But that's not really a goal; it's a wish. And people don't get what they wish for in life—they get what they picture. Once you've got that vision clearly defined, you can move ahead with an actual plan. As Dr. Henry Cloud likes to ask, "What is your desired future?"[29]

STEP TWO:
START YOUR PLAN AS EARLY AS POSSIBLE

It's important to think about the big picture and start your plan as early as you possibly can. I began planning for my financial future when I was twenty-four. I wish I would have started when I was eighteen. While it's normal to procrastinate, the longer we wait, the more it costs us in the end. **TIME is our greatest enemy!**

When we're in our twenties and just starting out, the future seems so far away. What's the rush? It's hard enough just trying to make ends meet.

Unfortunately, things don't get easier in our thirties, as job changes, work challenges, and kids tend to zap our time and energy. As a result, it's not until our forties or beyond that many of us even begin to seriously plot out a retirement strategy.

There's just no way around it. When it comes to retirement planning, waiting comes with a steep cost.

Let's say you hope to retire at sixty-five with a million-dollar retirement fund. Even if you had a tax-deferred plan with an 8% interest rate, here's what you'd need to contribute each month to reach that goal:

If you began at age 25, it would take	$286.45 / month
If you began at age 30, it would take	$435.94 / month
If you began at age 35, it would take	$670.98 / month
If you began at age 40, it would take	$1,051.50 / month
If you began at age 45, it would take	$1,697.73 / month
If you began at age 50, it would take	$2,889.85 / month
If you began at age 55, it would take	$5,466.09 / month

AND IF YOU BEGAN AT AGE 60... IT WOULD TAKE A WHOPPING $13,609.73 / MONTH!!

As you can see, the longer you wait, the harder it becomes to hit that million-dollar goal. You literally can't afford to put off planning for your financial future. **The only person who will take care of your older self ... is your younger self, and the sooner you begin, the better.**

STEP THREE:
PREPARE FOR THE UNEXPECTED

One of the biggest mistakes people make when preparing for retirement is that they plan for the idealized version of their future on a flat line.

YOUR PLAN

Unfortunately, that's now how life works. Unexpected things happen all the time. Life is full of unforeseen circumstances like lawsuits, disabilities, health scares, accidents, inflation, market risks, and family issues. **Prepare, don't predict. How reliable is your plan?**

REALITY

My mindset has always been to hope for the best but plan for the worst. Life can be unpredictable and throw curveballs your way. If you're not set up for the worst, your retirement plan may face serious problems. You'll be much better off preparing for reality instead of fantasy.

I had a client who worked as a Secret Service agent in Washington, D.C. His plan was to retire at age sixty-one. He had everything in place, and then the market crashed. This caused him to delay his retirement until age sixty-four, which was unfortunate because he ended up passing away at age seventy-one.

Another client started working for United Airlines when she was eighteen. She put $25 per paycheck into company stock, which eventually grew to $125,000. After spending forty-three years with the company, her pension grew to $7,500 per month. She seemed to be all set. Then suddenly, in 2002, United went bankrupt. Her account dropped to $0. The government took over her pension plan, and she now receives a mere $500/month.

"MY MINDSET
HAS ALWAYS
BEEN TO
HOPE FOR
THE BEST
BUT **PLAN
FOR THE
WORST**."

—PHIL BODINE

I'm a firm believer that you must have a solid defensive plan. I always say to have "MAXIMUM PROTECTION WITH THE LEAST AMOUNT OF COST." If you gathered all of my clients in a room, they would rather have a 100% chance of getting to 95% of their target wealth than take a 50/50 chance of getting to 100%. Would you agree?

To do this, you need to put guardrails on your retirement plan. Would you drive your car across the Golden Gate Bridge on a wet and windy day if the bridge had no guardrails? I think not. Building cushions and contingency strategies into your plan prevents you from being left out in the cold if the market crashes.

Many people do not have enough backup in their plans because of laziness or incompetence on the part of their advisor, frugality on the part of the firm, or ignorance on their part. It takes time and money to educate advisors on developing comprehensive plans for their clients. So, instead, firms like to create generalized, cookie-cutter templates, which, unfortunately, aren't specifically tailored to meet the individual needs of their client. Ideally, what we all want is an advisor with an all-inclusive approach.

And if you're looking for an easy-to-follow formula for allocating your money, in general, I usually recommend living by the **10-20-70 Rule:**

❶ Give 10% of your income to charity.

❷ Save 20% for retirement.

❸ Spend 70% on living expenses/lifestyle/ entertainment.

STEP FOUR:
DIVERSIFY WITH A PLAN FOR ALL SEASONS

Many mainstream financial institutions like to promote five sources of retirement income, which usually include things like Social Security, pension plans, IRAs, earnings, and asset income. This is fairly common, but in all honesty, you can do better.

Ideally, you want to have as many sources of retirement income as possible in case one dries up, a tax law changes, or the economy crashes. You never want to put all your eggs in one basket.

My good friend, John L. Smallwood, CFP®, runs a workshop called "Retire A.S.A.P. (As Safe As Possible)." He shares nineteen different sources of retirement income,[30] preaching that the best way to protect against unforeseeable obstacles is "to diversify income as much as possible."

The goal isn't necessarily to employ all nineteen options. But it is smart to broaden your investment horizon. It's like having several silos in your backyard, each with unique advantages. Each has different risks, different guarantees, and different tax treatments, and they're all at your disposal to tap into when you need them the most.

19 SOURCES OF RETIREMENT INCOME

1. Social Security

2. Pensions

3. Interest from Investments

4. Ordinary Dividends

5. Qualified Dividends (taxed differently)

6. Tax-Free Dividends

7. Whole Life Insurance Dividends and Cash Value

8. Capital Gains Income

9. Business Income

10. Royalties

11. Partnership Income

12. Real Estate Income

13. Reverse Mortgage

14. Immediate Annuity Income

15. Annuity Income

16. Roth Income

17. IRA Income

18. Principal Paydowns

19. Charitable Remainder Trust Income

Ultimately, retirement is all about transitioning from **"you working for money"** to **"having your money work for you."** And in that process, some of your income sources will be passive while others are active.

A common misconception about retirement is that when you retire, you will stop investing for your future. But those who are wise never stop investing. It remains an active part of nurturing true wealth. The income that you receive from your investments should always involve some sort of recirculation back into your plan. It's the very essence of the velocity of money.

Let me conclude with a story about a client who employed all four points I just outlined. He was a dentist who worked as a TMJ specialist making mouthpieces for the NFL Jacksonville Jaguars and the NHL Tampa Bay Lightning. He loved his profession and wanted to phase out of the working world rather than retire abruptly when he got older. His plan was to reduce down to a three-day workweek at age fifty, a two-day workweek at age fifty-five, and a one-day workweek by age sixty. To his credit, that's exactly how his life unfolded. Even though he had enough money saved to retire comfortably by age sixty, he continued working and disciplining himself to save so he could have more freedom as he got older. He considered his dental practice to be his absolute best investment and source of income. This man was so prepared that when the market tanked, his assets actually went up in value.

Now, that's what you call a man with a plan! He defined retirement on his own terms. He started early, laid a foundation, prepared for the unexpected, followed his vision, put disciplines in place, diversified enough to keep the market fluctuations from ruining his dream, and lived a fulfilled retirement on his terms—freedom, flexibility, and control. We should all be that prepared.

Peak Performance Tip #17

Start with the end in mind.

HOPE for the **BEST**,
but **PLAN** for the **WORST**.

EIGHTEEN

ANSWERS TO THE QUIZ AND THE PRINCIPLES BEHIND THEM

SOMETIMES THE QUESTIONS ARE COMPLICATED AND THE ANSWERS ARE SIMPLE.

—DR. SEUSS

Well, it's time to get down to business and reveal the answers to the quiz we took at the start of our journey together. But before we delve into the answers, I'd like you to take the financial gear quiz one more time using the knowledge you got from this book. Let's see if your financial understanding is any higher!

FINANCIAL GEAR QUIZ

TRUE	FALSE		
◯	◯	**1.**	Insurance companies want you to have the lowest deductible possible on your auto and homeowners insurance.
◯	◯	**2.**	A 15-year mortgage will save you more money over time than a 30-year mortgage.
◯	◯	**3.**	Term life insurance has the highest overall cost to you, the insured, over your life expectancy.
◯	◯	**4.**	You will be in a lower tax bracket at retirement.
◯	◯	**5.**	Tax deferrals, like IRAs and 401(k)s, are the most efficient way to accumulate wealth.

TRUE	FALSE		
○	○	**6.**	Life insurance is a good investment.
○	○	**7.**	The rate of return on home equity depends on the location of the home.
○	○	**8.**	A life insurance company allows you to borrow from your life insurance contract.
○	○	**9.**	Given the insured's age and the size of the desired death benefit, the life insurance company determines the maximum amount of premium to be paid.
○	○	**10.**	A life insurance company is buying your risk when you purchase a life insurance contract.

How do you think you did this time? Were you more confident? Did you easily answer some questions and still struggle with others? Let's turn the page and learn what the answers are and what you can take away from them. I hope this all makes more sense to you and you'll feel ready to make some financial strategy changes that will take you into *OVERDRIVE!*

QUESTION #1:

Insurance companies want you to have the lowest deductible possible on your auto and homeowner's insurance.

The answer is **TRUE**. Remember, insurance companies want you to have the lowest deductible possible because they can charge you more premiums. But when you run the numbers, you're not getting the most bang for your buck.

The difference between the price of a low deductible and a high deductible is significantly more than the benefit would justify. You'd be better off choosing the higher deductible and putting the extra money you would have spent into an account where you can control it, not to mention watch it grow. And then, if an accident does happen, you've got your own account to draw from to get your vehicle back on the road. You are essentially self-insuring for the deductible.

The goal is to keep the big picture in mind. You want to protect yourself from financial catastrophes, not financial inconveniences. A $1,000 deductible won't devastate your financial future. The same holds true for homeowner's insurance. Select a plan that offers the most protection for the least cost.

KEY TAKEAWAY

Don't overpay for peace of mind.

QUESTION #2:

A 15-year mortgage will save you more money over time than a 30-year mortgage.

The answer is **FALSE**. While most financial institutions want to convince you that a 15-year mortgage will save you thousands, you have to remember their ulterior motive. They want to control as much of your money as possible. And a 15-year mortgage means higher payments (from you to the bank). The more money they get from you, the more they can loan back out to others. Essentially, you're giving the bank the opportunity to capitalize on your money, which is not a smart move for the wealthy-minded person.

Yes, you save the interest you would have paid over that 15-year period, but you forego the interest you could have earned elsewhere.

Remember, the bank owns the money in the home, not you. So, the more you dump into higher payments, the less control and safety you will have with your money. And the better it will be for the bank.

Another reason you want a 30-year mortgage is because it allows you to **leverage inflation and increase your cash flow to your benefit**. Your payments today won't seem nearly as high in thirty years.

Plus, your home simply isn't a great investment vehicle. It's not liquid. It's not meant to storehouse cash. It's not safe from loss of principle. There is no rate of return. Higher payments reduce your tax benefits, and there's no real sound exit strategy.

It's true that many financial entertainers encourage the 15-year mortgage because they like to promote getting out of debt as soon as possible, playing to your emotions. However, sound economics requires making decisions based on more than simply emotions.

KEY TAKEAWAY

*Not all debt is bad debt.
It's the duration of the mortgage that's
important, not just the interest rate.*

QUESTION #3:

**Term life insurance has the highest overall cost to you,
the insured, over your life expectancy.**

The answer is **TRUE**. Even though term insurance seems much cheaper than whole life insurance, there are four hidden costs that most people never consider.

First, there's the actual cost of the contract, which appears inexpensive until you consider that it builds no equity within the contract. You're essentially rolling the dice and betting that you will die before the contract runs out. And when it does run out, there's nothing left for you. To keep the contract in force, you have to keep reapplying and gaining pre-approval for coverage.

Second, the rates increase as you get older. In fact, term policies are designed to outprice the customer. Insurance companies want you to eventually cancel your contract so they won't be obligated to pay a death benefit. You spend years forking over thousands of dollars only to ultimately drop it and let the insurance company off the hook, leaving you holding the bag. And, by the way, it's an empty bag.

Third, the money you sink into a term contract is money you could have invested elsewhere. We're talking about opportunity cost. You want your dollars to work for you, not for someone else. It's a high price to pay for peace of mind, especially when you consider you're also paying for a product that will only lose value over time, not gain.

And finally, they seldom payout. Term insurance is a product that many people purchase and then never get to use. The eternal cost to your family and generations to come from losing the death benefit is almost incalculable. Imagine if everything you purchased in life worked like that. There are smarter ways to spend your money.

It's important to remember that term insurance is a better short-term strategy than a long-term strategy.

KEY TAKEAWAY

Less than 2% of term life insurance policies ever pay a death benefit.

The bitterness of poor quality remains long after the sweetness of low price is forgotten.

—Ben Franklin (via Bill McFadden)

QUESTION #4:

You will be in a lower tax bracket at retirement.

This is **FALSE**. The belief that you'll be in a "lower tax bracket at retirement" is a fallacy that financial institutions concocted in the late seventies/early eighties when the maximum federal tax rates were 70% to 80%. It was designed so they could sell government-sponsored plans to help you "save on your taxes."

HISTORY OF THE U.S. MARGINAL TAX RATES (1913–2023)

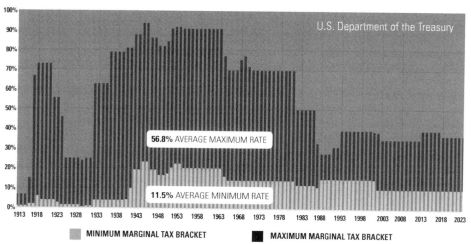

The reasoning seems sound. It's based on comparing your working years with your non working years. When you're working, you pay a lot of income tax. But when you're retired, and you've stopped receiving paychecks, your taxes should naturally go down, right? Seems to make sense.

Unfortunately, it's not that simple. For one thing, your children are now grown, so you no longer have dependents to write off. And if your home is paid off, you've lost the ability to write off the interest portion of your mortgage payments. And if you have money in a government-sponsored plan, there are huge tax implications.

KEY TAKEAWAY

If you are in a lower tax bracket at retirement, you didn't really plan for retirement. Or, you're dependent on someone else for income.

QUESTION #5:

Tax deferrals, like IRAs and 401(k)s, are the most efficient way to accumulate wealth.

The answer is **FALSE**. While government-sponsored plans are extremely popular, they are neither an efficient nor an effective way to invest your money.

These types of plans fail every principle of my **5-Way Test** for making wise and prudent financial decisions. They're not **liquid**. They offer no **safety**. The rate of return cannot be calculated. There are no real **tax benefits**. And the **exit strategy** is a disaster. Once again, tax deferral plans are great accumulators but poor wealth distributors.

"It's time to declare the 401(k) a **failure**. As the default plan of America, it just doesn't measure up...too much **risk**... if risk can be insured away, it ought to be done."

Eric Schurenberg
Editor-in-Chief CBS Moneywatch.com
May 2016

And remember, tax-deferred is not the same as tax-free. It simply doesn't make sense to postpone your tax obligations or tax calculations to a year in the future when the tax rates are much more likely to be higher than lower. This is not a winning strategy.

It's almost always smarter to pay the taxes as you go along at a **known** rate today (on the seed) than it is to get stuck with a major tax bill at the end, the **unknown** tax rate (on the harvest).

Like mortgage payments, the money is no longer yours. It belongs to the government. They call the shots, and you are at their mercy. Remember, **you owed the tax the day you made the deposit**. The government loans you the tax to compound on their behalf at your expense.

There are so many better ways to invest your money. The goal is to have a happy ending, not a heartache ending.

Truly wealthy people have very little, if any, of their net worth locked up in qualified plans because they know better. Or they employ financial advisors who know better. When we have Ted Benna, the founder of the 401(k), looking back and declaring that he created a "monster," it should be obvious there are much better investment options.

KEY TAKEAWAY

*Government-sponsored plans
do not build or create wealth.*

QUESTION #6:

Life insurance is a good investment.

The answer is **FALSE.** Life insurance is a **CONTRACT,** not an investment. This is **CRUCIALLY IMPORTANT** to understand.

If it were an investment, it would be taxed! But since it is a contract, it shouldn't even be compared to other investments. Technically, it should be viewed as a **tax-efficient alternative asset class** that enhances your portfolio.

Why is this important? If, for some reason, the government someday decides to change the current tax laws and begin taxing life insurance cash value and the death benefit, all existing policies would be grandfathered, and the inside buildup would not be taxed. It falls under the ex post facto law, which states that new laws cannot apply to people operating before the new law was passed.

As things currently stand, a properly designed life insurance contract can become a flexible, risk-free, tax-free, flow-through entity for accumulating assets. It can provide every opportunity you need to invest in stocks, bonds, real estate, and all other investment options used by typical financial advisors. Most importantly, it lets you control your money as you see fit.

QUESTION #7:

The rate of return on home equity depends on the location of the home.

The answer is **FALSE**. The return on home equity is always the same. Zero. In and of itself, home equity has no rate of return. We somehow believe that when the value of our house goes up, we suddenly have a rate of return.

But that's not how it works. Equity has no rate of return when it's locked inside the house. It doesn't matter if your home is paid off or you haven't made your first payment. The home will appreciate or depreciate regardless of how much money you've paid into it.

This is the reason it's not smart to pay off your home. If your money is trapped inside your house, it's not earning any money. It's simply dead and idle dollars.

When we run this option against my **5-Way Test**, we determine it's not a wise and prudent financial decision. We've just established that the **rate of return** is nil. So, is it **liquid?** Not really. If your money is tied to your home, the money's not really yours. You either have to sell the house to get your money, or you have to go back to the bank and pay them interest to get your money.

Is it **safe?** If an earthquake, flood, fire, hurricane, or tornado destroys the neighborhood, or you lose your job, you don't want your money tied into your home. Having your money in a liquid account is much safer.

Are there **tax benefits?** The more money you sink into your home, the less you are able to write off. Why would you want to eliminate one of your biggest tax advantages?

Is there an **exit strategy?** You may think you have one, but there will be variables outside of your control when it comes to selling your home.

KEY TAKEAWAY

You're in a safer position with money outside the home than with the equity being tied up inside the home.

Don't be debt-free and broke!

QUESTION #8:

A life insurance company allows you to borrow from your life insurance contract.

The answer is **FALSE**. If you have cash value in your life insurance, you can borrow **AGAINST** it but not **FROM** it.

When you borrow against your equity, the cash value and the death benefit are used as collateral. If you fail to repay the loan, the loan balance is subtracted from the death benefit at the time of death. When you borrow against the cash value and the death benefit, the equity within the contract continues to grow uninterrupted, as if nothing has changed.

Compare that to the fallacy of compound interest, which, contrary to popular belief, is not the eighth wonder of the world. For that theory to work, your money must stay put in the plan. But the miracle of *uninterrupted exponential tax-free compounded growth* is the secret. And that's what borrowing **AGAINST** your contract allows you to do. It permits you to keep your equity compounding on your behalf.

KEY TAKEAWAY

*A **properly structured life contract** should be the foundation of protection and should serve as a productive place to storehouse cash.*

QUESTION #9:

Given the insured's age and the size of the desired death benefit, the life insurance company determines the maximum amount of premium to be paid.

The answer is **FALSE**. While both age and benefit amount play a role in determining the price of your premium, it's not the insurance company that determines the volume of money allowed into the contract. Life insurance is regulated by state insurance commissioners. The government establishes the maximum amount that can be paid for an insurance contract.

KEY TAKEAWAY

*If the government limits the amount of money allowed to be put into a life contract, it must be **REALLY GOOD**!*

QUESTION #10:

A life insurance company is buying your risk when you purchase a life insurance contract.

The answer is **TRUE**. When you buy an insurance contract, you are signing a contract whereby both parties have mutual obligations that are enforceable by law.

You are agreeing to make payments, and the insurance company is agreeing **to buy/assume** your risk. They are legally obligated to pay the benefit if death happens while the contract is still in force. Insurance companies are experts at managing long-term risk.

In actuality, you're not really buying anything from the life insurance company because the death benefit is guaranteed to be greater than your deposits. No wonder Malcolm Forbes said,

"Buy as much life insurance as possible." [31]

KEY TAKEAWAY

Whole life insurance is the only insurance guaranteed to payout.

So there you have it! If you got half of them right, I'd say you did well. The questions in this quiz were intentionally designed to make you think and begin to reassess some of the cultural norms. The truth is that wealthy people don't follow the typical road map. They're driving on the autobahn in a completely different gear. And now that you're privy to some of their concepts, my hope is you'll begin employing some of them yourself as you begin your own journey to the world of true wealth.

NINETEEN

COURAGE & DISCIPLINE

EVERYONE WANTS TO WIN, BUT NOT EVERYONE WANTS TO PREPARE TO WIN.
—BOBBY KNIGHT

Wealth in Overdrive® was written to present a lifetime of economic acceleration principles, procedures, and processes for a more predictable outcome. My desire is to lead you to choose the lesser-traveled, narrow financial road to a better quality of life over the deceptive, often-traveled, bumper-to-bumper wider road that leads to nowhere.

Many of you are probably familiar with Henry David Thoreau's famous quote that states, "The mass of men lead lives of quiet desperation."[32] It's based on an observation that most people live empty lives caused by unfulfilling work, lack of leisure time, and/or misplaced values. The majority of people go through life asking themselves questions like, "Do I really want to do this?" or "Do I feel like doing that?" The problem is, you'll never get the right answers if you continue to ask the wrong questions. When it comes to finances, it's much smarter to ask yourself questions like:

* What's important to me about money?
* What do I hold most sacred in life?
* What do I like to do when I'm not working?
* What are my three most important financial objectives in order of priority?
* If money were no issue, what would I do with my life?
* What's the one thing that challenges me the most about money?
* What's something really important to me that I don't get a chance to talk about very often?
* Who do I rely on for financial advice, and are they credible?
* If I was given $1 million, where would I invest it?
* What is the number one thing I want to be remembered for by my family?
* What are the consequences if I don't plan for my future?

These are value-based questions that cut to the chase about what's really important. When you learn to focus on what matters most, you can lead with purpose, not fear or passivity.

Many people have asked me the difference between what we do and most other typical financial advisors. The chart below summarizes how we at Wealth in Overdrive® differentiate our exclusive process from the typical "main street" approach.

WEALTH IN OVERDRIVE® PROCESS VS	TYPICAL "MAIN STREET" APPROACH
1. **Strategy-oriented:** Based on time-tested principles and financial philosophies proven to build wealth.	1. **Product-oriented:** Focus is primarily on buying certain "products" or portfolios.
2. Optimizes your full wealth potential.	2. Just meets your needs and goals.
3. Assumes the "worst case" scenario—"Hope for the best, prepare for the worst."	3. Assumes no-change, best-case scenario.
4. Cost-recovery and cost-effective.	4. No cost-recovery methods.
5. Encourages increased cash movement and a continual flow of money.	5. Encourages a "hold" strategy where assets remain stagnant and locked in place.
6. Control over money at all times.	6. Relinquishes control to banks and financial institutions.
7. Promotes 401(k) alternatives and IRA alternatives that avoid or minimizes current and long-term tax implications.	7. Promotes maximum contributions to 401(k)s and IRAs and postpones long-term tax consequences.
8. Focused on recovering of lost opportunity costs and taxes.	8. Focused on rate-of-return.
9. Pursues wants and dreams.	9. Meets needs and goals only.
10. Macro-economic (big picture) based—We view your whole personal economy.	10. Micro-economic (vacuum) based—The focus is on your "portfolio."

"STRESS IS A SIGNAL THAT **SOMETHING NEEDS TO** CHANGE, SUFFERING IS WHEN WE DON'T MAKE THE **CHANGE**."

– BILL CRAWFORD

In a nutshell, the Wealth in Overdrive® approach is where you'll find optimum financial potential, more protection against economic threats, the least amount of cost, less risk, and pay fewer taxes.

I once got a call from a prospective client. He was the Chief Operating Officer (COO) of a well-known national company, and he had just chosen a financial planner nine months earlier after interviewing six others. Most introductory calls I have with new clients will last roughly fifteen to thirty minutes. This guy grilled me for nearly an hour and a half. As we wrapped up, he said he wanted me to meet his wife, who happened to be both a business owner and a scientist. I invited them to my home to create a more comfortable atmosphere. Once they arrived and we moved past the pleasantries, I began probing into what mattered most to each of them. Twenty minutes into my inquiries, his wife stopped me mid-sentence and looked at her husband. "This is what we've been looking for," she said. "He's asking the right questions!"

One of the biggest compliments to my business is that my former wife is still one of my clients. After we divorced, she interviewed a few different advisors but ended up coming back to me eight months later and said, "Phil, will you please manage my money? I've interviewed a bunch of idiots who have no idea what they're doing." She was smart enough to know the difference between typical planning and the principles in *Wealth in Overdrive*®.

If you can continue to return to your values and lead with what matters most, you will succeed. Albert Einstein once said, **"Try not to become a man of success, but rather try to become a man of value. He is considered successful in our day who gets more out of life than he puts in. But a man of value will give more than he receives."**[33]

While the strategies mentioned in this book may have made rational sense, they may also appear out-of-the-ordinary, counter-cultural, and even downright scary.

Let's be honest. It's hard to break away from the status quo. It takes thought. It takes courage. It takes discipline. It takes action!

The winners of the world are those who consistently make wise choices and stay the course in seeing them through. When it comes to wealth, winners have the courage to take the first step and the discipline to keep taking additional steps until this process becomes a habit and a natural part of their mindset.

One of my favorite stories is about a client who happens to be a doctor. He and his wife already had four children of their own, but they wanted to expand their family by adopting two little girls from Haiti. Even though they both worked and made good money, their assets were tied up and unable to be liquidated in time to fulfill their dream. In typical real-world investing scenarios, that would have been the end of the story. But as clients of mine, they were exposed to a different way of investing that allowed them to utilize the **5-Way Test (Liquidity, Safety, Rate of Return, Tax Benefits, Exit Strategy)**. Thank goodness they had the courage and discipline to restructure and reposition their finances in a way that gave them the access to capital they needed immediately. Their value-based way of living forever changed the lives of everyone in their family.

What you can accomplish when you add courage and discipline to your values is incredible. I have another client who was driven by a desire to spend more time with his children. He courageously borrowed and self-financed $150,000 against his contract so he and his wife could purchase a flower shop in Southern California. After eight years of hard work and discipline, they sold their busi-

"THE BIGGEST OBSTACLE TO ACHIEVING ANY GOAL IS ALWAYS... YOU!"

—PHIL BODINE

ness for $1.8 million. They're now living the dream, enjoying all kinds of time with raising their family. And they are even looking to open another flower shop in Chicago!

I've had other clients who have revamped their businesses. Some have traveled, and others have fulfilled adventures. Knowing how to access capital easily was foundational, and understanding their WHY was crucial. But having the courage, applying the discipline, and changing their mindset were the real keys to making their dreams become their reality.

Probably my favorite example of courage and discipline comes from a parable Jesus told in the Bible. You can find it in Matthew 25:14–30. It's called the "Parable of the Talents." Allow me to share a condensed, paraphrased, and modernized version for you.

A company CEO prepared for an extended trip. He called his employees together and delegated responsibilities. To one, he gave $50,000; to another, $25,000; and to a third, $10,000, based on their abilities. Then he left.

The first two employees immediately went to work and doubled their business owner's investments, while the third, out of fear, dug a hole and carefully buried his $10,000.

When the boss eventually returned, the first two reported their results. The CEO replied, "Nice work! You two shall be promoted within the company."

However, when the owner questioned the third man, he was greeted with, "Sir, I know you have high standards. I was afraid to disappoint you, so I hid your money in a safe and secure place. Here it is, just like it was when you gave it to me."

The boss was furious. He replied, "What a waste of time and talents! You could have at least put it in the bank and gained interest! Take the $10,000 and give it to the guy who optimized the most." And then he commanded that the "play-it-safe" employee be fired!

As you can see, the story doesn't end well for the man who is timid and passive. The easiest thing to do in life is nothing. The second easiest thing to do is to drift with the crowd and get caught in the current. But anything worthwhile takes courage and discipline. And that's especially true with finances. Bring the future into the present so you can fix it **NOW!**

The biggest obstacle to achieving any goal is always … YOU! Take the keys and this road map I've given you in this book, and get to work—no more excuses! It's time to shift your wealth and quality of life into *Overdrive!*

You cannot go back and change the beginning, but you can start where you are and create a better ending.

−C. S. Lewis

If you would like to subscribe to the **Wealth in Overdrive**® podcast, keep up to date with future events and **Wealth in Overdrive**® workshops, or set up a one-on-one consultation with one of our registered team members, simply scan the QR code below.

"FORGIVENESS DOESN'T EXCUSE THEIR BEHAVIOUR. FORGIVENSS PREVENTS THEIR BEHAVIOR FROM DESTROYING **YOUR HEART**."

— BILL CRAWFORD

EPILOGUE

EXPERIENCING FREEDOM

TO FORGIVE IS TO SET THE PRISONER FREE
AND DISCOVER THAT THE PRISONER
WAS YOU.

—LEWIS B. SMEDES

I consider it a privilege to share my life and the financial wisdom I've acquired. However, I'm doing you a disservice if I leave out one last crucial element that will kick your life and wealth into overdrive.

Financial advisors are a dime a dozen. Some are very knowledgeable and well-educated. Others are extremely intelligent and gifted with amazing communication skills. But no matter how brilliant or trained someone is, eventually, they will experience setbacks in life. Their responses and lessons learned from those setbacks are key elements to developing their true character.

This is important because a financial advisor is the macro manager of your financial team (see page 232). They are a confidant who you trust with your hard-earned money. And it is vital that you feel comfortable with their disposition as a person.

At the beginning of this book, I talked about my upbringing and how it formed my core beliefs. And while I've had a successful career, I've had more than my share of setbacks. How I responded to those difficulties helped shape me into a man of much deeper conviction. Allow me to divulge more of my personal story.

The year was 2000. I was well into my career. I was movin' and groovin', developing clientele, and growing my business. I was soaring higher than a kite! I was unstoppable. In fact, I thought I was invincible! Or so it seemed.

It was at that time that my wife of six years informed me she had been having an affair behind my back and was filing for divorce. I was devastated.

If you've never experienced this type of tragedy firsthand, it's really difficult to accurately describe the pain and rush of emotions that instantly cut you to the core. I was in shock. I was mad. I was sad. I was hurt, frustrated, and angry! I felt violated and betrayed. I felt like someone had sucker punched me. My entire world had just been turned upside down.

They say that divorce, in many ways, is harder than death. That was certainly the case for me. For the next ten months, I attended countless meetings where I watched our divorce attorneys battle back and forth. It was mentally grueling and emotionally exhausting.

When the legal dust finally settled, the physiological repercussions were just beginning. I was completely depleted and found myself experiencing a debilitating grief like I had never known before. That's a long way from the invincible feeling I'd had ten months earlier. I used to think nothing could bring me to my knees. But divorce did. And I fell hard.

If you remember earlier, I touched on an element of planning that you rarely hear financial advisors discuss—**Forgiveness**. Like the gentleman I mentioned at the beginning of the book who felt his family would never forgive him because of the loss he incurred as the steward of the family retirement plan. I've met so many people over the years who have created such a mess with their money they almost become paralyzed. They are so overwhelmed that they walk around like financial zombies.

And that's where I was, not with my finances and business but with my personal life. I felt totally defeated and didn't know where to begin. With clients, it was all about helping them take an honest look at their situation and then teaching them to forgive their past mistakes so they could move forward. When they did that, it became freeing. This forgiveness step was crucial, but it sure seemed a lot easier with money than with marriage.

Even though I grew up in church and had heard a lot about forgiveness, the truth is, I really didn't know **HOW** to forgive. As a kid, I learned to say "I'm sorry" when I disobeyed. But in my current circumstances, it all seemed quite different. Just saying or feeling sorry felt incredibly inadequate.

Fortunately, a friend of mine invited me to attend a program at church called "Divorce Recovery." I remember scoffing at him and telling him that I didn't need any help. I was fine and would get through this "divorce thing" on my own. So I didn't go. I deceived myself into thinking that time would heal all wounds.

"UNFORGIVENESS IS AN ACID THAT DOES A **GREAT DEAL MORE DAMAGE TO THE VESSEL** IN WHICH IT IS **STORED THAN THE OBJECT ON WHICH IT IS POURED**."

—AUTHOR UNKNOWN

That didn't dissuade my friend from pursuing me. For the next month or so, he continued to encourage me to attend. I finally relented. It was a Wednesday night when I found myself sitting at home alone with nothing to do. So I decided to give it a try. And then I went back the next week. And then the next. And the next. In the end, I learned more in that twelve-week class than I did from any college course I had ever completed. They covered depression, mental health, spiritual health, grief, anger, and reconciliation. It was all so therapeutic. But it wasn't until week thirteen that a sobering new topic was introduced—**Forgiveness**.

A pastor named Harold Graham taught that session. He was one of the most unassuming men I had ever met. Raised in a rural setting, he had a way of communicating that was incredibly blunt yet down-to-earth. Even though his words were piercing, I found it hard not to like a man with such a kind heart, gentle spirit, and passion for helping others.

Pastor Graham began by telling a story that struck me so hard I can still recall it quite vividly to this day. He had just transitioned from working as a commercial pipe fitter to a licensed pastor. He shared that he was two weeks into his new position as a pastor when a woman walked into his office looking for some pastoral counseling. In their second session, she finally admitted that she had been raped hundreds of times by multiple people in her past. Pastor Graham sat there listening and stunned, with no idea what to do other than offer her a box of Kleenex.

It was at that moment that he heard a voice telling him to "go to the chalkboard." The voice was so loud and so clear that he literally thought there was someone else behind him in the room talking to him. When he turned around, he saw no one. Shocked and confused, he thought to himself, "I don't understand. Go to the chalkboard?" As the woman was talking, he heard the voice a second time. This time, it replied, "Understanding is mine, obedience is yours." Harold thought, "This sounds a little bit like God."

Then he looked at the woman and said, "Do I have your permission to go to the chalkboard? I believe God has something to share with you on that chalkboard." She gave him permission.

Having no inkling of what was to follow, it wasn't until he picked up the chalk that he immediately felt the urge to start writing. It came to him fast as he scribbled furiously. For the next forty-five minutes, he unleashed an entire lesson about forgiveness. It was as if God downloaded His infinite wisdom about forgiveness straight to the chalk in Harold's hand. The woman was mesmerized as he spoke about how forgiving her perpetrators for the evil acts they committed against her would lift the heaviness of bondage from her spirit.

After the woman left, Pastor Graham spent the next two hours slumped in his chair, staring in disbelief at the chalkboard and everything he had written.

The next day was the launch of his new ministry, teaching others about the power of forgiveness. He did this for the next thirty-two years, walking thousands of people through the process of learning how to forgive.

After sharing that story, he had my attention. The class that night lasted three-and-a-half hours. It's no exaggeration when I humbly state that it changed my life forever. I went home and did exactly what he told me to do.

I took out a legal pad and prayed for God to help me identify every single person I could think of who had ever wounded or

"WHEN YOU **FORGIVE** SOMEONE, YOU TAKE THEM **OFF YOUR HOOK** AND PLACE THEM **ON** GOD'S HOOK."

—AUTHOR UNKNOWN

wronged me. My list included people who took advantage of me and people who had called me names.

Then I prayed and asked specifically what I needed to forgive each person for. Next to their names, I documented their offenses. It should be no surprise that the person at the top of my list was my soon-to-be ex-wife.

There were a lot of painful things I needed to forgive her for. I had to forgive her for the affair. I had to forgive her for the entire legal mess. I even had to forgive the man she cheated with, and I didn't even know his name. The list went on and on.

Surprisingly, I found myself adding my mother to my list for things she had said and done to me in the past. I discovered a lot of deep-seated anger, hurt, and resentment from years ago that I had buried far below the surface.

When I finished scribbling, my list contained fourteen names and nearly two pages of offenses. Now came the hard part: *I needed to forgive them.*

I reread my DivorceCare notes and found a prayer of forgiveness in the back of my notebook. I prayed that prayer (included as **Appendix One** after this section) and inserted the name of every single person and every single offense on my list. In all honesty, it was the most cathartic experience of my life as it purged my psyche of hundreds of negative emotions that had subconsciously been burdening my soul.

Living with bottled-up resentment has a profound impact on how we conduct our lives. And most of the time, we don't even realize it. Grudges weigh us down and make us bitter and angry. They eat us up from the inside out. By the time I finished praying, my pages were splattered with tears, but I felt an instant sense of peace as if a huge weight had been lifted from my chest and shoulders. And that night, for the first time in months, I slept like a baby. I was able to experience a peacefulness like I'd never known. I was a changed man and could finally begin to heal and move forward. All of a sudden, my future looked brighter than my past.

I don't know the significance of this, but exactly three days later, my doorbell rang at 9:30 p.m. I opened the door, and to my surprise, there stood my soon-to-be ex-wife, crying. I invited her in, and we had a wonderful conversation. And then she said two words I had never heard her say to me before: "I'm sorry."

It's such a simple phrase, yet it holds tremendous magnitude. At that moment, I knew God was real. **When I prayed that prayer of forgiveness over everyone on my list, I gave God permission to act on my behalf.** Little did I know that within days, I'd be witnessing God's convicting power right in front of my very own eyes.

I'd love to tell you that we immediately reconciled and lived happily ever after. But the truth is, three months later, our divorce was finalized, and we each went our own separate ways. Apparently, God had different plans for me. Part of His plans was to begin sharing my newfound freedom with others by becoming a facilitator with the same divorce recovery class that changed my life. (For more information, visit www.divorcecare.org.)

The people I met and the stories I heard were astounding. One of the most profound memories I have comes from the time I spent with a fifty-year-old man who shared his experiences with his abusive mother with me. The hurtful insults she hurled at him as a child continued to impact his psyche for decades. I couldn't help but notice he always wore long sleeves, which seemed odd during the heat of summer. In fact, he wore long sleeves every week in our class. And then, one day, I discovered why when we prayed together. In the middle of his prayer, he muttered the words, "And I forgive my mom for putting out her cigarettes on my arms when I was a kid." It caught me so off guard that I was moved to tears. It was such a powerful, life-changing moment. He walked out of that room, a free man, and the next time I saw him he was wearing short sleeves.

Another time, I was at the gym using the elliptical machine when I realized the woman working out right next to me happened to be a longtime acquaintance. Shortly after we started chatting, she went off on her soon-to-be ex-husband. She was spewing venom all over the place. What he did to her was incredibly hurtful. On the very day she was in the hospital about to give birth to their first child, he informed her of the "newfound love in his life" and said he wanted a divorce.

From that moment on, she made it her mission to tell everyone about how she had been wronged by her ex-husband and wronged by everyone else in his family, as well. I looked at her and said, "Sounds like your bedroom is a busy place at night."

"WTF does that mean?!!" she exclaimed.

I replied, "You're carrying your ex-husband, your ex-husband's mom, your ex-husband's brother, your ex-husband's sister-in-law, and your ex-husband's mistress with you to bed every night in your mind."

She immediately broke into tears. She had no idea what unforgiveness was or how it had taken root in her life. So I asked her if she'd like me to help her find freedom from all the weight and bondage she was carrying around. This was the start of a new chapter for her. Once she actually learned how to forgive, it was like being released from a prison cell, and she was finally able to move on with her life.

Usually, the sequence of events over time that leads to a downward spiral occurs in this order:

* An event happens that leads to hurt.
* Hurt leads to anger.
* Anger leads to hate.
* Hate leads to bitterness.

Never get caught in the trap of bitterness, **for BITTERNESS KEEPS US MARRIED TO YESTERDAY.**

What most people don't realize is that forgiving someone doesn't excuse their behavior. It prevents their behavior from destroying your own heart. When you forgive someone, you take them off *your* **hook and place them on** *God's* **hook.**

FORGIVENESS IS A GIFT YOU GIVE YOURSELF, not the other person. Without forgiveness, you carry the pain, bondage, hurt, anguish, grief, and brokenness around like a ball and chain. And that's a heavy load to carry everywhere you go. However, when you truly surrender it to God, you become a free person.

No one wants to live their lives burdened by such suffering. Real change is heart change. It can be hard and messy. But it's always worth it. And I'm living proof. My spiritual assignment is to defeat the powers of darkness of unforgiveness.

I once heard someone say, "Forgiving someone doesn't excuse their behavior. It prevents their behavior from destroying your heart." I believe this to be absolutely true. I've experienced it first-hand.

I share all this because my story may help you understand that I am as human as the next person. I'm no superhuman. I put my pants on one leg at a time, like everyone else. I've learned to really care about each and every client as a person. And isn't that what most people really want in an advisor—someone who genuinely cares?

My point is, character matters. It's been said, "Don't hire a coach based on how he reacts after the big victory. Hire a coach based on how he responds after a devastating defeat." If you understand how a person handles life's challenges, you will have a much better idea of what to expect in the long run.

In the end, true wealth isn't about the money or what you accumulate. It's about who you become and how you live your life. In the forty years of working with people, I've discovered that I am most fulfilled by helping others with their money and lives. It's my hope that by writing this book, I've been able to do the same for you.

Forgiveness is the greatest gift you can give yourself.

—Maya Angelou

IN MEMORIAM

REVEREND
HAROLD GRAHAM
1953-2021

THE FORGIVENESS PROCESS

EVERYONE THINKS FORGIVENESS IS A LOVELY IDEA UNTIL HE HAS SOMETHING TO FORGIVE.
—C. S. LEWIS

If there's one thing I've learned, it's impossible for me to forgive others more than God has forgiven me. What would happen if you forgave the people who hurt you in your past? I know from firsthand experience that forgiveness is not easy. But bitterness and unforgiveness are magnetic, and clinging to them is like drinking poison. It only hurts you in the end. My advice is to be quick to forgive!

For your benefit, I've included a list of what forgiveness **IS NOT**, what forgiveness actually **IS**, how to work through the **PROCESS** of forgiveness, and two **PRAYERS** that have made a world of difference in my life. I pray it does the same for you.

Forgive
Ephesians 4:32

Forgiveness Is NOT...

... a feeling ... Most people don't want to forgive;

... pardoning the offense or saying it was okay;

... forgetting (as in forgive and forget);

... instant restoration of trust; `

... resuming the relationship without conditions or boundaries;

... minimizing the seriousness of the offense;

... an excuse for their behavior.

Forgiveness IS...

... a gift you give yourself, not the other person;

... an intentional decision you make to let go of resentment and anger;

... releasing God to work on your behalf;

... bringing their balance to zero;

... giving up the right to hate them forever for what they did;

... releasing yourself from punishing the offender;

... releasing you from keeping records;

... taking the offender off your hook and putting them on God's hook;

... getting your heart right with God.

HOW TO WORK THROUGH THE FORGIVENESS PROCESS

❶ Find a quiet place with a notepad and pen.

❷ Pray and ask the Holy Spirit to reveal to you people in your past who have wounded or offended you.

❸ Write down all of the names that come to your mind, making plenty of space between each name.

❹ Then pray and ask the Holy Spirit what, specifically, you need to forgive them for.

❺ Write down the specific offenses beside each name. Try to take your time. See examples of how to do this on the next page.

❻ Insert the name and the offenses in the prayer below. Pray through each name until you are finished.

❼ Rinse and repeat as often as necessary.

Here are two examples from two people who attended one of my forgiveness workshops. I hope you find them useful to you in your process.

EXAMPLE 3

First Name Cliff   Dad
                          (Relationship)

1. verbal abuse   16. not listening
2. not protecting me   17. not showing love
3. unrealistic expectations 18. hated mom
4. selfish   19. did not trust God
5. controlling   20. not respecting me
6. ungodly example   21. being fake — phony
7. made me afraid   22.
8. belittled me
9. name calling — stupid lazy
10. bad example of husband
11. abuse of mom
12. exposed me to pornography
13. instilled low self-esteem
14. anger
15. did not model forgiveness

EXAMPLE 2

First Name Nadine   Ex
                          (Relationship)

1. betrayal   16. false Reporting to police
2. Rejection   17.
3. name calling   18.
4. put downs   19.
5. insults   20.
6. you call yourself a man 21.
7. adultery   22.
8. hate   23.
9. won't admit wrong   24.
10. lies   25.
11. deception   26.
12. selfishness   27.
13. drug abuse   28.
14. alcohol abuse   29.
15. violence — hit me   30.

32

PRAYER FOR FORGIVING OTHERS

Father in Heaven, thank you for sending your Son, Jesus, to die on the cross for the forgiveness of my sins so that I might truly live. As a step of faith, I choose to trust you for my healing, and that begins with me asking for and accepting the forgiveness you offer.

I have done things that I'm not proud of. In fact, I'm even embarrassed by them. They have hurt me, and they have hurt others. I've never really been taught how to forgive. I've lived most of my life stuffing pains and wrongdoings inside and burying them down deep. And now it's time to dig them up and hand them over to you.

I now, today, confess to you that I have nursed grudges against

_____

(person's name)

and have used my pain to rationalize my own sin. I have

_____

(hated, grown bitter, resented, judged, disliked, avoided,
wished harm, etc.)

I have been so hypocritical. I've kept a mental record of their wrongs against me while I have excused my own wrongs against them. I have not truly forgiven until now.

I ask you to forgive me. I ask you to clean up my mess and make me whole again.

With your help, I freely choose to declare before you that I forgive

_____

(person's name)

specifically for the following:

-

-

-

-

-

God, I transfer

_____'s

(person's name)

offense against me over to you. It is now yours, not mine. **I DON'T WANT TO CARRY IT ANY LONGER.** I also ask that you would convict them of their offenses in your own way and in your own time so that they will confess before you as well and surrender their heart to you. Make them whole again, too.

Thank you, Lord, for the good work you continue to do in me,

Amen.

PRAYER FOR SALVATION

If you are at a point in your life where you would like to accept the Lord Jesus Christ as your Savior, you can do that by praying this simple prayer. After praying, will you please reach out to me at phil@philbodine.com? I would love to hear from you about the biggest decision you made in your life. If it isn't quite the time for you to make this eternity-changing, life-altering decision, I simply pray you think about what all this means and remain open to God's leading.

Dear Lord,

I know that I am a sinner who needs a Savior. I am coming to You as I am. Please forgive me for every sin against You. I choose right now, to turn away from my past. Take my life and make it Yours. I believe in my heart and confess with my mouth that Jesus Christ is Lord. He died for me and rose again. And I ask Him now to come into my heart. I make Him MY Lord and Savior. Please send Your Holy Spirit to help me live for Him all the days of my life. Thank You, God, for sending Your Son to pay the price I owed for my sins. Thank You for Your grace and mercy!

In Jesus's name. Amen!

70 BENEFITS OF PERMANENT LIFE INSURANCE WITH A MUTUAL COMPANY

The benefits described below are "strategy" concepts that demonstrate the power and flexibility of owning Permanent (Whole) Life Insurance with a **MUTUAL** Life Insurance company.

LIVING BENEFITS:

1.   The cash value can be accessed by withdrawals (to basis) or loans providing a **TAX-EXEMPT** income.

2.   There is no income tax on earnings if the policy is structured correctly and maintained properly.

3.   Provides liquidity for emergencies and other needs.

4. The yield is above average as compared to other "fixed income" instruments.

5. The asset is safe with guarantees: guaranteed death benefit, cash value, and premiums.

6. The asset is available as collateral.

7. Loans are available on a favorable basis.

8. Offers possible liability lawsuit protection against claims of creditors in many states.

9. Flexible policy features after a short period of time.

10. Contributions (premiums) can be flexible.

11. No premium increase, but it can decrease or offset with dividend options.

12. No maximum contribution limits like qualified plans, but they may have insurability limits.

13. No age 72 required minimum distribution (RMD) requirements.

14. Source of funds for emergencies, education, and retirement.

15. Contributions are systematic, creating a committed savings habit.

16. Contributions will continue in the event of disability if a Waiver of Premium is included.

17. Eliminates the "need" for Term Insurance and its related costs (LOC).

18. Enhanced tax benefits as tax rates may rise.

19. Makes non-income-producing assets produce an income.

20. Accelerated benefits riders offer cash before death if chronically or terminally ill, thus protecting other assets from consumption and "spend down" requirements.

21. The need for life insurance never goes away, not even with sufficient assets, because life insurance is a wealth-maximization asset.

22. Tax-exempt loans have no effect on your credit score.

23. Accumulated cash value will not negatively affect FAFSA calculations for college, whereas 529 balances will!

RETIREMENT BENEFITS:

24. Distributions at retirement can be "tax-favored" if designed and structured correctly.

25. No minimum distribution requirements at age 72.

26. Maximum distributions are permitted.

27. Makes income-producing assets provide greater retirement income.

28. Not subject to stock market fluctuation losses on liquidation (except Variable Life), thus reducing market or interest rate risk on asset portfolios.

29. Not subject to early retirement restrictions: age 59 ½ rules.

30. Vesting is immediate.

31. Provides increasing income during retirement rather than fixed income.

32. A lifetime tax-favored income stream is available with various options.

33. No annual tax return requirement, reducing income taxes throughout retirement.

34. Not subject to ERISA, DEFRA, TEFRA, OBRA, or IRC 400 series regulations.

35. Not subject to compliance penalties or fines like qualified plans.

36. No termination requirement hassles.

37. Simple to initiate: requires no attorney, CPA, or government approval.

38. Not subject to employee scrutiny or publicity.

39. No employee participation requirement.

40. Not subject to annual actuarial studies/costs.

41. Diminishes concern over running out of money.

42. Can receive a life settlement for immediate cash.

43. Works well for a retiree who dies too soon or lives too long.

44. Distributions and withdrawals don't cause taxation of Social Security benefits when designed correctly.

45. Distributions and withdrawals don't cause "higher Medicare" premiums for higher net-worth taxpayers when designed correctly.

46. Can be used in business situations to reward key employees and retirement incentives.

A PERMISSION SLIP FOR:

47. Possible pension maximization strategies.

48. Pay down of assets (principle and interest over lifetime).

49. Possible value in planning a reverse mortgage.

50. Collateral for a private loan.

51. Long-term care benefits if the policy contains LTC riders, plus it can replenish "spend down" assets in long-term care planning.

ESTATE PLANNING:

52. Assets may be assigned to a trust.

53. Fully eligible for the marital deduction.

54. Not subject to probate, if structured correctly.

55. No publicity at death.

56. Results in estate growth.

57. Can be used to pay taxes on large IRA/Qualified Plan distributions at death, making "stretch IRA" options over 10 years better.

DEATH BENEFITS:

58. You **OWN** that number.

59. Proceeds are received in cash.

60. Proceeds are received **TAX EXEMPT** when structured correctly.

61. Possession of this asset is an expression of love and concern to family, business associates, and charities.

62. Proceeds can be received as a lifelong annuity income stream.

63. Provides for payoff of personal, mortgage, and business debts at death.

64. Provides cash to keep a business afloat until the family can sell the business or make other arrangements.

65. Provides cash for the continuation of the family's plans when a key family member is deceased.

66. Death benefits could "replenish" money spent on medical expenses paid prior to death.

67. Death benefits could "replenish" money spent on convalescence/nursing home costs prior to death.

68. Provides an asset for special needs children.

69. Death benefits can increase with PUAs and dividend options if structured correctly.

70. Can enhance the estate for heirs when other assets are illiquid.

SUMMARY

The above 70 benefits can be discussed and illustrated during planning discussions and strategy meetings. Some of these benefits **DO NOT** apply to other types of life insurance such as Term Insurance, Variable Life, Equity-Indexed Life, or Universal Life. A few of the benefits may apply to these other types of insurance. Only Whole Life with a Mutual Life Insurance company offers all these benefits when structured and designed correctly under the advice of a trained life insurance professional.

ABOUT THE AUTHOR

Phil Bodine is the founder and CEO of **Wealth in Overdrive**®. He's been working as a wealth strategist since 1989, helping executives and small business owners create and optimize their full wealth potential.

After earning a Bachelor of Science degree in Business from Indiana University, Phil spent nineteen years establishing and serving a client base in Fort Wayne, Indiana. In 2008, he moved his office to Roseville, California, to expand his practice as a nationwide financial advisor, author, and guest speaker. His **Wealth in Overdrive**® workshop has changed the lives of thousands throughout the country.

Phil is a husband, father, and grandfather. His outside interests include volleyball, golf, fishing, and travel. He serves various charities through Bayside Church and is partnered with Convoy of Hope®. His passion for marketplace ministry is teaching others the "Freedom of Forgiveness."

To connect with Phil Bodine, visit **WealthInOverdrive.com** or scan the QR code to schedule a consultation, subscribe and listen to the latest episode of the **Wealth in Overdrive**® podcast, see upcoming events and **Wealth in Overdrive**® workshops, or through social media.

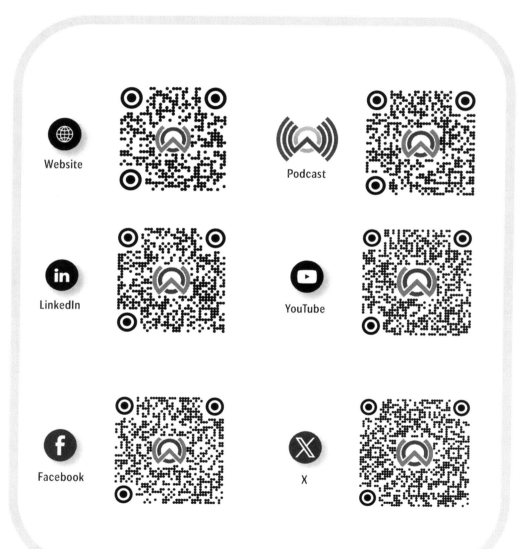

RECOMMENDED RESOURCES

Live Your Life Insurance by Kim Butler

Tax-Free Wealth by Tom Wheelwright, CPA

Killing Sacred Cows by Garrett B. Gunderson

What Would Billionaires Do? by Garrett B. Gunderson
(What Would the Rockefellers Do?)

Rich Dad Poor Dad by Robert Kiyosaki

Goals: Getting What You Want Most at Work and Home by Jud Boies

Confessions of a CPA by Bryan Bloom, CPA

Soar: You Were Meant to Live for So Much More by Zoro

Maria's Scarf: A Memoir of a Mother's Love by Zoro

The New Retirement Savings Time Bomb by Ed Slott, CPA

Little Red Book of Selling by Jeffrey Gitomer

The AND Asset by Caleb Guilliams

It's Your Wealth—Keep It by John L. Smallwood, CFP®

DivorceCare Recovery Group (www.DivorceCare.org)

NOTES

Chapter 2

1 Chicago. Miller, Bennett. 2011. Moneyball. United States: Columbia Pictures.

2 Ron Marshall, "How Many Ads Do You See In One Day?" September 10, 2015, Redcrowmarketing.com, https://www.redcrowmarketing.com/blog/many-ads-see-one-day/.

3 "Personal Savings Rate for October 2023," U.S. Bureau of Economic Analysis, October 3, 2023, https://www.bea.gov/data/income-saving/personal-saving-rate.

4 Grant Cardone, "I am not paying taxes ever again," YouTube, May 14, 2022, https://www.youtube.com/watch?v=vL4L8NpqTeY.

5 Mark Twain, *Following the Equator: A Journey Around the World*, reprinted from the original 1897 first edition (SeaWolf Press, 2022).

Chapter 5

6 John Tukey (1962). "The Future of Data Analysis," *Annals of Mathematical Statistics*, 33 (1): 13.

7 Google search: "McDonald's 2024 price of hamburger," accessed June 12, 2024.

Chapter 6

8 "S&P 500 Total Returns by Year," www.slickcharts.com/sp500/returns.

Chapter 10

9   Kelley Holland, "For millions, 401(k) plans have fallen short," March 23, 2015, CNBC.com, https://www.cnbc.com/2015/03/20/l-it-the-401k-is-a-failure.html#:~:text=Benna%2C%20who%20is%20often%20called,said%20in%20a%202013%20interview.

10   Sarah Max, "The Inventor of the 401(k) Thinks It Has Gone Awry," November 16, 2018, Barron's Retirement Q & A, https://www.barrons.com/articles/401-k-inventor-ted-benna-says-the-retirement-plan-has-gone-awry-51555759800.

11   Bryan S. Bloom, CPA, *Confessions of a CPA: The Truth About Life Insurance* (West Conshohocken, PA: Infinity Publishing, 2013).

Chapter 12

12   Joshua Sherrard, "How A 'Rich Person Roth' Can Help You Minimize Taxes, Fees, and Volatility," Forbes.com, December 10, 2020, https://www.forbes.com/sites/forbesfinancecouncil/2020/12/10/how-a-rich-person-roth-can-help-you-minimize-taxes-fees-and-volatility/?sh=2b4bb2635a61.

13   www.USdebtclock.org.

14   "Wage Statistics for 2022," Social Security Online, https://www.ssa.gov/cgi-bin/netcomp.cgi?year=2022.

15   Robert Frank, "More than 40% of U.S. households will owe no federal income tax, down from last year, according to a new analysis," October 28, 2022, CNBC.com, https://www.cnbc.com/2022/10/28/more-than-40percent-of-us-households-will-owe-no-federal-income-tax-for-2022.html#:~:text=An%20estimated%2072.5%20million%20households,from%20the%2056%25%20in%202021; https://www.taxpolicycenter.org/model-estimates/tax-units-with-zero-or-negative-federal-individual-income-tax-oct-2022/t22-0132; https://www.taxpolicycenter.org/model-estimates/tax-units-with-zero-or-negative-federal-individual-income-tax-oct-2022/t22-0133.

Chapter 13

16   NOTE: Achieving the CFA designation is the equivalent of passing the Bar in Economics in the financial world.

17 Wade D. Pfau, *Safety-First Retirement Planning: An Integrated Approach for a Worry-Free Retirement*, Retirement Researcher's Guide Series (Vienna, Virginia: Retirement Researcher Media, 2019).

Chapter 14

18 Natalie Robehmed, "Mystery Billionaire Buys Record-Breaking $201 Million Life Insurance Contract!" March 14, 2014, Forbes.com, https://www.forbes.com/sites/natalierobehmed/2014/03/14/mystery-billionaire-buys-record-breaking-201-million-life-insurance-policy/?sh=754d3a2d1e3c#:~:text=An%20unnamed%20Silicon%20Valley%20billionaire,in%20the%20low%20digit%20millions.

19 "Ed Slott's Retirement Freedom," PRNewswire.com, February 24, 2022, https://www.prnewswire.com/news-releases/new-show-ed-slotts-retirement-freedom-now-airing-on-public-television-nationwide-301489427.html.

20 Ed Slott, "Your 5 Best Arguments for Life Insurance Besides the Death Benefit," Wealthforlife.net, Denver Nowicz, https://wealthforlife.net/2017/07/your-5-best-arguments-for-life-insurance-besides-the-death-benefit/.

Chapter 15

21 Polly LaBarre, "How To Lead a Rich Life," February 28, 2003, Fastcompany.com, https://www.fastcompany.com/46097/how-lead-rich-life.

22 General Accounting Office Report, "Tax Policy: Tax Treatment of Life Insurance and Annuity Accrued Interest," January 1990, 27.

23 General Accounting Office Report, "Tax Policy: Tax Treatment of Life Insurance and Annuity Accrued Interest," January 1990, 27.

24 Wade D. Pfau, Ph.D., CFA, Michael Finke, Ph.D., CFP®, "Integrating Whole Life Insurance into a Retirement Plan: Emphasis on Cash Value as a Volatility Buffer Asset," © 2019 Wealth Building Cornerstones, LLC.

25 "Benefits of Integrating Insurance Products into a Retirement Plan," © 2021 Ernst & Young, LLP. US Score no. 12521–211 US.

Chapter 16

26   Kim Kiyosaki, "Money Affects Everything," October 15, 2021, https://www.youtube.com/watch?v=kZXu6fiwMrQ.

27   Wade Pfau, "The Retirement Researcher Manifesto—Part 2," https://retirementresearcher.com/the-retirement-researcher-manifesto-part-two/.

28   AZ Quotes, "Red Adair Quotes," https://www.azquotes.com/author/68-Red_Adair.

Chapter 17

29   Dr. Henry Cloud, "The Audit: Your Values, Vision, Mission, Goals and Time Will Define Your Life," Boundaries.me, https://s3.amazonaws.com/kajabi-storefronts-production/sites/19226/themes/2149727/downloads/orAaK4VTtiipD8fT4poQ_The_Audit_-_Boundaries_dot_Me_-_Dr_Henry_Cloud.pdf.

30   John L. Smallwood, CFP®, "Retire ASAP: As Safe As Possible Participant Guide," January 8, 2019, https://www.amazon.co.uk/Participant-Guide-Retire-ASAP-Possible/dp/1792104545.

Chapter 18

31   James Flanigan, "Malcolm Forbes' Lesson on Estate Taxes," LATimes.com, March 4, 1990, https://www.latimes.com/archives/la-xpm-1990-03-04-fi-2867-story.html.

Chapter 19

32   Henry David Thoreau, "Walden, 1854," 3, https://pdcrodas.webs.ull.es/fundamentos/ThoreauWalden.pdf.

33   The Sundheim Group, "A Brief Visit with Einstein," May 10, 2018, from "Death of a Genius," article written by William Miller of LIFE Magazine, May 2, 1955, https://www.sundheimgroup.com/a-brief-visit-with-einstein/.